TOP **10**

MALLORCA

W0113962

CONTENTS

MALLORCA

INTRODUCING

Mondragó beach

WELCOME TO
MALLORCA

Whether you want to hike the mighty Tramuntana mountains, explore medieval villages or relax on fabulous beaches under cerulean skies, Mallorca has something for every traveller. Don't want to miss a thing? With Top 10 Mallorca, you'll enjoy the very best the island has to offer.

The dreamy coves and sweeping bays that line its sun-kissed shores have put Mallorca firmly among the Med's most popular holiday hot-spots. But leave the coast behind and you'll see why this Balearic island's natural beauty extends well beyond its beaches. Mallorca is scattered with show-stopping sights, ranging from the soaring canyons of Torrent de Pareis and the jagged Península de Formentor to spectacular subterranean cave systems, some of which include underground lakes like magical Coves del Drac. Many enchanting

Platja Portals Vells

towns and villages pepper Mallorca's timeless landscape, too, from pretty Valldemossa, where the composer Frédéric Chopin once spent a winter composing preludes, to picture-postcard Deià and its breathtaking sea-meets-sierra views.

Of course, Mallorca isn't all wild scenery and sleepy towns. Any trip to the island should include a deep dive into the buzz and bustle of the cosmopolitan capital, Palma. Hop between its medieval Old Town and the contemporary boulevards around La Rambla, and explore the impressive centuries-old sights of La Seu, Castell de Bellver and Palau de l'Almudaina, before trading history

for avant-garde art at Es Baluard. Time your visit with one of the many local *correfoc* festivals such as Festes de Sant Sebastià, and you're in for a raucous treat of dancing demons and fire-fuelled revelry. When you're ready to escape the city, hop on the antique train that trundles north to the lush citrus-scented valley of Soller and immerse yourself again in Mallorca's bucolic paradise.

So, where to start? With Top 10 Mallorca, of course. This pocket-sized guide gets to the heart of the island with simple lists of 10, expert local knowledge and comprehensive maps, helping you turn an ordinary trip into an extraordinary one.

THE STORY OF
MALLORCA

Mallorca's transformation from rustic backwater to tourism trailblazer has been a roller-coaster ride. From conquests by Romans, Moors and Catalans to suffering bouts of cultural repression, turbulent times are nothing new to this Balearic isle. Here's the story of how it came to be.

The First Settlers

Historians agree that the island's first settlers arrived from the Iberian Peninsula during the third millennium BCE, though little is known about them. Archaeological remains, including flint tools and primitive pottery, suggest that these inhabitants were hunters and shepherds. From this era emerged the Talayotic culture, in around 1300 BCE, who were named for their characteristic defensive towers known as "talayots". This was an advanced society that constructed numerous settlements across Mallorca, though their dominance wouldn't last. The island's strategic location on ancient trading routes attracted a variety of settlers during the first millennium BCE, including the Phoenicians and Carthaginians. The latter would go on to occupy Mallorca until they were defeated by the Romans in the Second Punic War (218–201 BCE).

Conquest and Subjugation

Despite this victory, the Romans didn't remain in Mallorca. Only in 123 BCE, after Carthage had been destroyed, did the Roman Consul Quintus Metellus arrive with an armed force and after two years of resistance, the Talayotic islanders were pacified and integrated into the Roman Empire. The Roman era, marked by the advent of olive oil and wine production, as well as the construction of two major towns (the modern capital Palma, and Pollentia, whose ruins can be seen near Alcúdia), saw relative stability. But after five centuries, the decline of the Roman Empire opened the gates to invasions, first by the Vandals in 425 CE and then the Byzantine Empire in 534 CE. The Byzantines remained until the 8th century, when its own decline was met by pirate attacks, Norman Vikings and the Emirate of Cordoba, foreshadowing the Moorish occupation.

Depiction of the Roman invasion of Mallorca

A painting of the Christian reconquest of Mallorca

The Moorish Occupation and Christian Reconquest

After years of incursions and piracy by Arab seafarers, the Moors finally launched an invasion in the early 10th century, marking the start of over 300 years of rule. The Moors transformed Mallorca: introducing new crops, such as oranges, lemons and rice, developing the economy and growing Palma into a cosmopolitan city. Their legacy is still visible today, in most place names and in both architecture and gastronomy.

Eventually, Moorish piracy gave King Jaume I of Aragon an excuse to mount an invasion. In September 1229, his army landed at Santa Ponça and, after several bloody battles, entered Palma on 31 December 1229, annexing the island to his Kingdom of Aragon. Jaume set about removing Muslim vestiges, constructing churches and encouraging Christian Catalan settlers. Under Jaume and his successors, Mallorca flourished as an independent kingdom, crowned by the construction of the Castell de Bellver and Convent of Sant Francesc. This halcyon period ended abruptly in 1344 when Catalan forces, angered by this autonomy, invaded and crushed all resistance. Once again, Mallorca was part of the Kingdom of Aragon and remained so until 1479 when the union between Castile and Aragon united Spain. Despite the veneer of stability, these centuries were marked by piracy, plague and uprisings, most notably in 1521 when a revolt led to the deaths of many nobles.

Moments in History

1300 BCE
The start of the Talayotic period, characterized by the construction of lookout towers and settlements from huge rock slabs.

123 BCE
Mallorca is conquered by the Romans under Quintus Caecilius Metellus, who names the island Balearis Major.

902 CE
The island is conquered by the Moors during the Umayyad Caliphate's expansion, starting three centuries of Muslim rule.

1229
King Jaume I invades Mallorca and vanquishes the Moors to claim the island for the Kingdom of Aragon.

1479
Mallorca is incorporated into the newly created Kingdom of Spain, formed through the union of the Kingdoms of Castile and Aragon.

1701–14
The Spanish War of Succession does not directly damage Mallorca, but results in the crowning of Felipe V, and an invasion of Mallorca shortly after.

1808–13
The Peninsular War against Napoleonic forces leads to an influx of Catalan refugees to Mallorca.

1936–39
The Spanish Civil War unfolds, ending in victory for Franco's Nationalists and 36 years of Fascist dictatorship.

1983
The Balearic Islands gain autonomy within Spain allowing for self-governance and the promotion of local culture and language.

2023–24
After visitor numbers hit a record 14 million, activists launch anti-tourism protests across the island.

Spanish War and Repression

Thanks to its ties to Spain, Mallorca was engulfed by the events of the Spanish War of Succession (1701–1714). The island did not see any fighting but the support of many Mallorcans for the defeated Charles of Austria would have far-reaching consequences. After peace had been secured, the new king, Felipe V, landed with a military force in 1715 and forced Mallorca to submit in under a month. Although Felipe was able to finally end the pirate scourge, he also stripped away many of the rights and privileges islanders had enjoyed for centuries, including its government, and banned the Catalan language.

Forging Modern Mallorca

The island's fortunes continued to fluctuate into the 19th century. The Napoleonic Wars in Spain led to several waves of Catalan refugees pouring into Mallorca and much social and economic unrest, exacerbated by bouts of famine and plague. Yet gradually things did improve and shoots of modernity were soon evident. By 1837, a regular steamship service connected Mallorca to mainland Spain and the first railway between Palma and Inca was opened

Fighting during the Spanish War of Succession

General Francisco Franco during the Spanish Civil War

in 1875. Alongside this was a nascent tourist industry, headlined by the visit of the famous composer Frédéric Chopin and his partner, the French writer George Sand, and a resurgence of Catalan culture, expressed through the rejuvenation of the native dialect, Mallorquin, and the Modernista architecture of Antoni Gaudí, among others.

Tourism and Civil War

By the early 20th century, tourism was on the up. The first hotel opened in 1903, and by 1935 Mallorca was receiving around 40,000 foreign tourists per year and had a regular commercial air service to Madrid. But just a year later, this industry would be curtailed by the Spanish Civil War (1936–1939). A Republican force attempted to invade Mallorca in August 1936, but were bloodily rebuffed as the island threw its support behind General Franco's Fascist forces. After this, Mallorca was largely untouched by fighting and instead played host to the Italian air force, sent to support Franco's Nationalists.

During Franco's subsequent dictatorship, Mallorcan culture and language was again heavily suppressed. Instead the island's potential as a cash cow was realized and it was heavily promoted as a tourist destination once more. The ensuing tourist boom, which continues to this day, dramatically reshaped local culture, economy and geography into what it is today, with new resorts and towns such as Palma drastically enlarged to accommodate the influx of tourists.

Mallorca Today

Franco's death in 1975 ushered in an era of regional resurgence, typified by the revival of Catalan culture and, in 1983, the establishment of the Balearic Islands as an autonomous community within Spain. Yet the modern era has fundamentally continued to be defined by tourism, a boon to the economy but a costly one at that. Mallorca's success in this field has fuelled the unfettered proliferation of hotels and holiday rentals, leading to spiralling house prices and increasing concerns for the environment. Widespread protests by locals have occasionally spilled into anti-tourism sentiments. While most Mallorcans agree that the island could not survive without tourism, locals are increasingly demanding political action to curb the worst excesses to preserve the island for future generations.

TOP 10
EXPERIENCES

Planning the perfect trip to Mallorca? Whether you're visiting for the first time or making a return trip, there are some things you simply shouldn't miss out on. To make the most of your time – and to enjoy the very best this wonderfully varied island has to offer – be sure to add these experiences to your list.

1 Ride the Tren de Sóller and tram

Whisk yourself from Palma (p94) to Sóller (p36) aboard the century-old train and tram. The train (p36) takes you past some of Mallorca's best scenery, such as historic viaducts and tunnels, while the tram trundles to the port, along the narrow and crowded streets of Sóller.

2 Stroll through Palma

The island's capital, Palma (p94) is a cosmopolitan concoction of history and modernity with a great dining scene and café culture to boot. A walk here is a journey through history, from the Moorish city to the medieval Old Town and right up to the Modernist buildings influenced by Antoni Gaudí.

3 Discover hidden beaches and bays

Mallorca is famous for its beaches but a little extra effort will reward you with stretches of pristine and empty beaches. Kayak to the clear waters at Cala Beltrán or hike in the Llevant Peninsula Nature Reserve (parcnaturaldellevant.blogspot. com) to find picturesque hidden bays.

4 Hike in the Tramuntana Sierra

With peaks of over 1,000 m (3,300 ft), this UNESCO-designated mountain range guarantees spectacular views and hikes along cobblestone paths and past beautiful bays perfect for a dip. To see all of Mallorca's varied landscapes, try the 140-km (85-mile) GR221 route.

5 Indulge in art

Mallorca has an eclectic arts scene with fabulous collections to explore. Start with the former studio and home of artist Joan Miró at the Fundació Miró Mallorca *(p28)*, see sacred art at Museu d'art Sacre *(p97)* and find the latest trends at Es Baluard *(p60)*.

6 Visit a cave

Subterranean lakes, towering rock formations and giant caverns are all found in Mallorca's hidden world of 200 caves. See stunning stalagmites and stalactites in the Coves de Campanet *(p116)* or take a boat ride on the lake in the millennia-old Coves del Drac *(p46)*.

7 Take a boat trip

Get a unique perspective on the island from the waters around Mallorca. Hire a private boat or take a cruise to get off the tourist trail and find those harder-to-reach bits of untouched coast, beaches and coves that make a trip truly magical.

8 Tour picturesque towns

Mallorca bursts with beautiful towns and villages fit for a postcard, whether it's the artists' village of Deià *(p104)*, fairy-tale-like Valldemossa *(p32)* or the cobbled lanes of Fornalutx *(p102)*. Be sure to visit on market day when towns come alive with activity.

9 Drink in a winery

Ever since the Romans introduced grapes, Mallorcans have had a love affair with wine. Today over 70 vineyards produce all kinds of vintages and many offer tours and tastings. There's even a designated Wine Route *(binissalemdo.com)* for 14 vineyards in the Binissalem area.

10 Visit Cabrera Maritime National Park

Hop on a boat and head to this stunning protected island group *(p30)* 18 km (11 miles) from Mallorca. You'll find perfect hiking trails, clear waters brimming with marine life and migrant birds on rugged cliffs. You might even see dolphins.

ITINERARIES

Exploring historical sites, hiking pine-scented sierras, cooling off in iridescent waters: there's a lot to see and do in Mallorca. With places to eat, drink or simply take in the view, these itineraries offer ways to spend 2 days and 7 days on the island.

2 DAYS IN PALMA

Day 1

Morning

Start your two-day tour of Mallorca's capital at the city's most iconic landmark, La Seu cathedral (p22). Take in the soaring Gothic-style design of its exterior then venture inside to explore its chapels and portals, and spot the somewhat divisive Gaudí renovations. Upon exiting, pop across the road to admire the Moorish-inspired architecture of the grand Royal Palace of La Almudaina (p24). A couple of hours can be spent touring the historic medieval rooms and viewing the giant tapestries inside the palace, before a leisurely amble into the nearby S'Hort del Rei (p70) gardens with their pretty fountains and shaded walkways.

> 🚌 **TRANSPORT**
> A bike lane runs along much of Palma's seafront, passing many of the city's best sights. The route is largely flat and wide, making it a great option for beginners.

Afternoon

Stroll up Palma's broad boulevards, popping into boutiques on Passeig del Born and flower stalls on La Rambla, before lunch at Mercat D'Olivar (mercat olivar.com). Refuelled, head on to the Fundación Juan March (p98), a fabulous gallery showcasing modern Spanish art (including Miró, Picasso and Dalí) in a 17th-century mansion. Take a little time afterwards to soak up the stunning architecture in Plaça Major and Plaça de Cort (p86); the latter includes the town hall with its unusual façade. Continue south and walk along Palma's stunning promenade to the former fishing village of Portixol. It's a lovely spot for a dip and, when it's time for dinner, Restaurante Ola del Mar serves seafood good enough for Spanish royalty (oladelmar.es).

Day 2

Morning

Start your second day with a fancy breakfast buffet and panoramic views from Hostal Cuba's Sky Bar (hotel

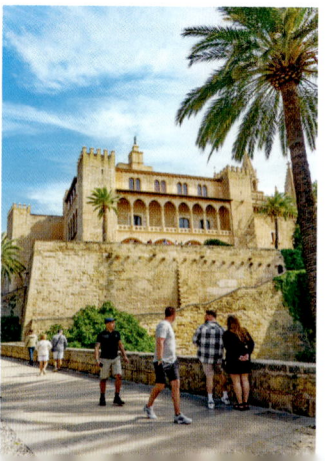

Looking up to the royal Palau de l'Almudaina

hostalcuba.com). Fuelled up, head out for a stroll around the fountains and gardens of Parque de sa Feixina (p71) before a visit to Es Baluard art gallery (p60), an excellent museum with a collection of over 800 works, primarily from the 20th century, and regularly changing temporary exhibitions. Spend a few hours marvelling at the art before heading on to the colourful Santa Catalina Market (p99) where you can soak up the lively atmosphere, sample some fresh produce and enjoy a tapas lunch at one of the stalls.

Afternoon

After lunch, head to the western edge of the city and the 14th-century Castell de Bellver (p26). Grab a bicycle from a Bicipalma (bicipalma.com) hire point (the nearest is at the corner of C/de Sant Magí and C/d'Espartero) and cycle over or enjoy the 40-minute walk. The castle is set atop a hill and offers breathtaking panoramas, particularly from the top of the castle. Take time to explore both the circular castle, with its excellent museum on the history of Palma, and the beautiful Bosc del Castell de Bellver

**A cheese and ham stall,
Mercat de Santa Catalina**

Park that surrounds the site. If you hang around till evening you might just get a perfect sunset over the bay. As night falls, stroll through pine forest to the Paseo Maritimo area for your pick of restaurants overlooking the marina – you can't go wrong with a pizza at Pizzería Ca'n Pelut (canpelut.es).

West Palma

- Sa Feixina Park
- Santa Catalina Market
- Hostal Cuba's Sky Bar ②
- Es Baluard
- Bosc del Castell de Bellver Park
- Pizzería Ca'n Pelut
- Castell de Bellver

0 metres 500
0 yards 500

- La Rambla
- Mercat D'Olivar
- Fundación Juan March
- Plaça Major
- Passeig del Born
- Plaça de Cort
- S'Hort del Rei
- Royal Palace of La Almudaina ①
- La Seu Cathedral

- Restaurante Ola del Mar
- Portixol

0 metres 300
0 yards 300

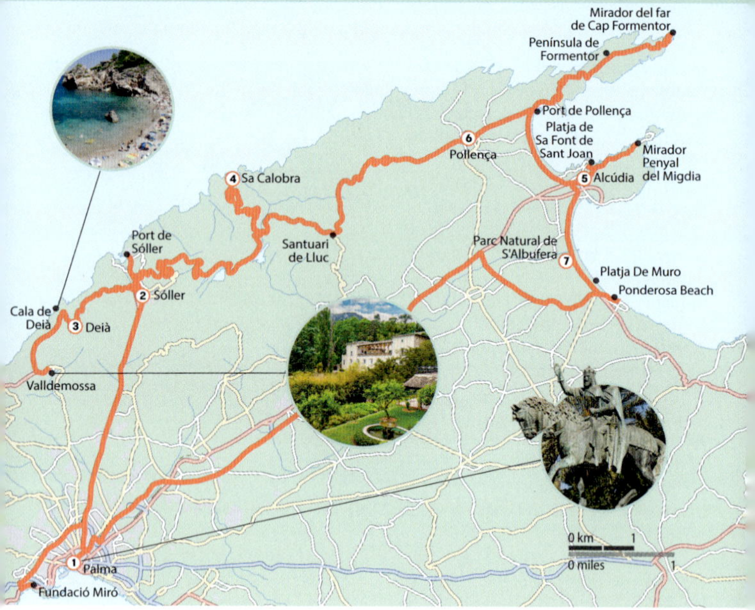

Mirador del far
de Cap Formentor

Península de
Formentor

Port de Pollença
Platja de
Sa Font de
Sant Joan

Mirador
Penyal
del Migdia

⑥ Pollença

⑤ Alcúdia

④ Sa Cobra

Santuari
de Lluc

Parc Natural de
S'Albufera

⑦

Platja De Muro

Ponderosa Beach

Port de
Sóller

② Sóller

Cala de
Deià

③ Deià

Valldemossa

0 km   1

0 miles   1

① Palma

Fundació Miró

7 DAYS

Day 1

Kick off your seven-day adventure in Palma's historic centre. The Museu de Mallorca (p95) is a good place to learn about Mallorca's heritage through art and artifacts, and this historical theme can continue with a visit to the nearby Arab Baths (p95), which highlight the Moorish legacy. After lunch, enjoy a stroll around the lake at Parc de la Mar (p98), soaking up views of La Seu (p22), before visiting the cathedral itself. Finish with a little retail therapy in Passeig des Born's quirky boutiques and a dinner of creative tapas at Tast Unión (p11).

Day 2

Board a bus (lines 46 or 47) west to visit the Fundació Miró (p28), a museum dedicated to the artist Joan Miró in his former home and studio. After, take bus 46 to Plaça d'Espanya and hop aboard the famous antique train to make the

Café patrons enjoying outdoor seating on Passeig des Born

one-hour trip from Palma to Sóller (p36). Stroll Sóller's historic lanes and visit the Jardí Botànic de Sóller (p71) before taking the vintage tram to Port de Sóller. Hike up to the Cap de Gros lighthouse (p37) and enjoy a leisurely dinner at Agapanto (p109).

Day 3

Today is a day to see Mallorca's pretty villages. Hire a car and head 20 minutes south to the village of Deià (p104), long associated with writers and poets. Pause at the Església de Sant Joan Baptista (C/ Reverendo Jerónimo Pons) and then walk past the stone houses to Cala Deià for a swim. In the afternoon, drive to nearby Valdemossa (p32). Soak up the beautiful architecture as you stroll along tiny cobbled streets, and visit the Real Cartuja monastery (p32), where the composer Chopin once stayed. Dine in Valdemossa before returning to Sóller.

> ### ⊙ VIEW
> Located roughly halfway between Pollença and Formentor beach, the sea–meets–mountain views from the Mirador de Es Colomer (p40) are among the island's most iconic.

Day 4

After breakfast head to Sóller market to pack a lunch of local produce for a beach picnic and swim under the soaring cliffs of Torrent de Pareis in Sa Calobra (p116). It's only an hour's drive but don't rush this scenic route (p74). Enjoy the picnic, then head to Mallorca's most spiritual site, Santuari de Lluc (p38), to see the Renaissance churches, Gaudí interiors and maybe hear the famous Blauets choir. Finish the day with a 40-minute drive to stay in Alcúdia (p44).

Day 5

If Alcúdia's twice-weekly market is on, start your day there – it's one of the largest in Mallorca. Then it's off to the remarkable Roman ruins of Pollentia (p44), a short walk from town, where you can check out the well-preserved amphi-theatre. The afternoon can be spent relaxing and snorkelling on Platja de Sa Font de Sant Joan. Or, adventurous hikers can tackle the Mirador Penya del Migdia hike with its stunning coastal views. To find the start, drive north from town and park at Ermita de la Victoria.

Day 6

Rise early and drive 20 minutes to the historic town of Pollença (p114). Wander its medieval alleys and climb the 365 steps of El Calvari (C/ Sense nom, 324) for views over the town. Devour top-notch tapas at Q11 (p119) to fuel an afternoon in the nearby Península de Formentor (p40). Start with a swim at

pretty Platja de Formentor (p69) before enjoying the spectacular drive to reach the lighthouse at the northern tip (note: from June to September you must use the shuttle bus, p40). It's a half-hour drive back to Alcúdia for one last night.

Day 7

After a stroll on Alcúdia's ancient walls, make the short hop south to the Parc Natural de s'Albufera (p114), the largest wetland area in the Balearic Islands and a haven for birdlife. It's best explored on two wheels so hire a bike from any of the local rental outlets. Finally, relax on one of Mallorca's finest beaches, Platja de Muro (p68), and eat a toes-in-the-sand lunch at Ponderosa Beach (Casetes des Capellans, 123), before making the hour's drive back to Palma.

Walking down stone stairs into historic Pollença

TOP 10 HIGHLIGHTS

Castell de Bellver

EXPLORE THE
HIGHLIGHTS

There are some sights in Mallorca you simply
shouldn't miss, and it's these attractions that
make the Top 10. Discover what makes each
one a must-see on the following pages.

Port de Sóller

Sóller Valley **6** Sóller

Deià Orient

5 Valldemossa

La Granja Santa Maria del Camí

Estellencs Consell

Ses Olleries

Sant Elm Palma La Seu: Palma Cathedral **1**

Andratx Castell de Bellver **2**

Fundació Miró Mallorca **3**

S'Arenal

Cala Blava

Sa Torre

Can Ripoll

Cap Blanc

Serra de

1 La Seu:
Palma Cathedral

2 Castell de Bellver

3 Fundació Miró Mallorca

4 Cabrera Maritime
National Park

5 Valldemossa

6 Sóller Valley

7 Santuari de Lluc

8 Península de Formentor

9 Alcúdia

10 Coves del Drac

Península de
Formentor **8**

Pollença

Badia de
Pollença

9 Alcúdia

7 Santuari de Lluc

Lluc

Crestatx

Tramuntana

Sa Pobla

Inca

Muro

Son Real

Badia
d'Alcúdia

Son Serra
de Marina

Cala
Mezquida

Llubí

Capdepera

Artà

Sineu

Son Servera

Petra

Sant Llorenç
des Cardassar

Cala Millor

Pina

Vilafranca
de Bonany

Manacor

Porto
Cristo

Algaida

10 Coves del Drac

Llucmajor

Porreres

Serres de Llevant

Felanitx

Cala Murada

Campos

S'Alqueria
Blanca

Sa Ràpita

Cala d'Or

Santanyí

Portopetro

Colònia de
Sant Jordi

Cala
Figuera

Na Gosta

4 Cabrera Maritime
National Park

0 kilometres   10
0 miles   10

LA SEU: PALMA CATHEDRAL

🚇 M5 🏛 Plaça de la Seu, Palma 🕐 Apr–Oct: 10am–5:15pm Mon–Fri, 10am–2:15pm Sat; Nov–Mar: 10am–3:15pm Mon–Sat 🌐 catedraldemallorca.org ↗

Palma's cathedral is an imposing pile, with its Gothic buttresses, finials and bosses. Legend has it that King Jaume I ordered its construction after a vow he made to God in 1230. Work began in 1306 and continued into the 1630s. The west façade was rebuilt after an earthquake in 1851, and Gaudí's controversial "Crown of Thorns" was added in the 20th century.

1 Portal del Mirador

The seaward, Gothic façade is the most spectacular side. Ornate buttresses surround an elaborate door. It was formerly called the Door of the Apostles but is now known as the Mirador (vantage point).

2 Bell Tower

The cathedral's enormous bell is set within a late medieval three-storey-high tower surmounted by a "crown of lace" – a perforated stone parapet with small pinnacles.

3 Gaudí Modifications

In 1904–14, the great Modernista architect Antoni Gaudí set about improving La Seu's interior, removing altars and installing electric lights. The controversial baldachin is actually only a mock-up – he never finished the final canopy.

4 Chapels

The aisles to either side of the nave are flanked by a series of chapels. The highlight is the Capella del Corpus

TOP TIP

The cathedral's roof terrace offers great harbour views. Book ahead for tours.

Stunning 14th-century Portal del Mirador

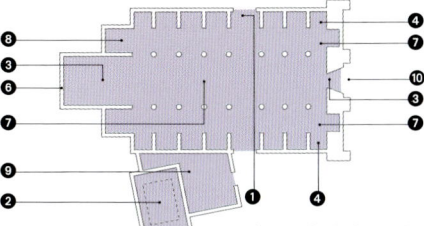

Palma Cathedral Site Plan

Gothic cathedral of La Seu

Christi, just to the left of the high altar and with a lovely carved altarpiece.

5 Portal Major
Although the cathedral is Gothic in style, the main door is the product of Renaissance artisanship. A figure of Mary is surrounded by objects symbolizing her purity.

GAUDÍ'S SOUNDING BOARD

Antoni Gaudí created an ingenious sounding board to ensure that the priest's voice would be projected throughout the immense cathedral. The wood-and-fabric creation sat above a pulpit until 1972, when new technologies rendered it obsolete and it was removed.

6 Rose Windows
A vibrant rose window at the end of the nave is the most notable of the seven (a few are blocked up). Some say the 20th-century "restoration" of the coloured glass was too strong.

7 Nave Columns
La Seu is one of Europe's tallest Gothic structures, and the sense of space in its interior is enhanced by elongated pillars that seem to fade away in the upper reaches of the nave.

8 Capella del Santíssim
Designed by renowned contemporary Mallorcan artist Miquel Barceló, the Chapel of the Most Holy features fine stained-glass windows and a large ceramic mural. The mural is based on the miracle of the Feeding of the Five Thousand, with images of teeming fish and rustic loaves.

9 Museum
Highlights of the cathedral's museum include some of La Seu's earliest altar panels, furniture, a polychrome wood sarcophagus and ornate reliquaries. The collection of Mallorcan Primitive paintings are particular standouts.

10 Exterior
From afar, La Seu seems to have more in common with a craggy mountain than it does with any European cathedral. The design reflects the might of its Christian founders.

Slender octagonal columns in the nave

Palau de l'Almudaina

1. Function of the Palace

Standing directly opposite La Seu, in an equally prominent position, the ancient Palau de l'Almudaina adds a lighter, graceful note to Palma's assemblage of civic buildings. Today, the royal palace is mainly used for legislative and military headquarters, but the royal family sometimes hosts ceremonies and state receptions here in the summer.

2. Building Style

An amalgam of Gothic and Moorish styles, the palace has a unique charm. Medieval towers have been topped with dainty Moorish-inspired crenellations. Refined windows and open, airy arcades also tell of an abiding Islamic influence.

3. Hall of Councils

The largest room on the ground floor takes its name, Salón de Consejos, from a meeting of ministers called here in 1983 by Juan Carlos I. There are 16th- and 17th-century Flemish tapestries, coats of arms and furniture.

4. Officers' Mess

The walls of this room are graced with beautiful 17th-century Flemish tapestries and genre paintings, some by a talented contemporary of Rubens.

5. Terrace and Banys Àrabs

Step onto the terrace for spectacular panoramic views. Then, back inside, peer into the remains of the Arab

Elegant interior of the Queen's Office

Baths. By means of mirrors, visitors can examine the three separate vaulted chambers below – one for hot, one for tepid and one for cold water.

6. Chapel of St Anne

This chapel's delicately coloured altar-piece, created in Barcelona in 1358, is a visual sonnet in sky-blue and gold.

7. Central Courtyard

Known variously as the Patio de Armas, the Patio de Honor and the Patio del Castillo, this central courtyard also evokes Moorish architecture, with its elegantly looping arches and central stand of palm trees. A small fountain incorporates a 10th-century lion sculpture from the original Islamic fort.

8. Queen's Office

The Royal Staircase to the upper floor leads to the Queen's Office, which has fine antiques, tapestries and paintings.

9. King's Rooms

Decorations in these rooms include huge 17th-century Flemish tapestries, bronze statuary and Neo-Classical paintings, as well as Spanish Empire furniture with glittering ormolu decoration.

10. Gothic Hall

This remarkable room, noted for its huge pointed arches, is used to hold official receptions. Admire the fine 16th-century Flemish tapestry (on the back wall) depicting the Siege of Carthage.

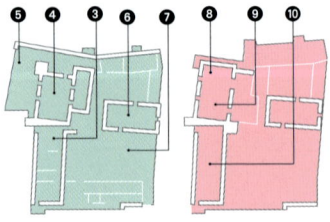

Key to Floorplan
 Ground floor
First floor

Palau del'Almudaina Floorplan

MALLORCA'S UNIQUE ARCHITECTURAL HERITAGE

TOP 10
TYPICAL FEATURES OF
TRADITIONAL HOUSES

1. Kitchen fireplace

2. *Clastra* (main patio)

3. Cisterns

4. *Tafona* (oil press) and mill room

5. Defence tower

6. *Capilla* (family chapel)

7. Stone walls, floors and sometimes ceilings

8. Vaulted ceilings

9. Wood beams

10. Motifs derived from Islamic, Gothic, Rococo, Italian Renaissance, Baroque, Neo-Classical or Modernista styles

Mallorca has a good supply of quality stone, which has been easy to quarry, and a ready supply of timber in the forests of the Serra de Tramuntana. Both have been used throughout the centuries to create homes, palaces and more. The prehistoric Talayotic peoples used stone for their villages – Ses Païsses near Artà *(p121)* is a great example. The Romans also built stone buildings, like the ruins of Pollentia on the edge of Alcúdia *(p44)*. The Moors, who governed the island from the early 10th to the 13th century, specialized in ornate timber decoration – the best surviving example is at the Jardins d'Alfàbia *(p50)*. After the Christian reconquest of Mallorca in 1229, Jaume I and his successors used stone for all key structures, including religious buildings, the most beautiful of which is La Seu *(p22)*. In the early 20th century, wealthier Mallorcans favoured the Spanish version of Art Nouveau – Modernista – a style used in several buildings in Palma *(p94)* and Sóller *(p36)*.

The Gothic Palau de l'Almudaina, built from Mallorcan stone

CASTELL DE BELLVER

C4 · Carrer Camilo José Cela, s/n, 3 km (2 miles) W of the city centre, Palma · 971 735065 · Apr–Sep: 10am–7pm Tue–Sat, 10am–3pm Sun & hols; Oct–Mar: 10am–6pm Tue–Sat, 10am–3pm Sun & hols

Over 700 years old, this castle was once a grand 14th-century fortress, a royal summer residence and later a prison. Surrounded by pine woods, it has stunning views (*bellver* means "lovely view" in Catalan) over Palma Bay. It is now home to a small history museum.

1 Views
Go to the top of the towers for 360-degree views, including the hills and sea to the west and mountains to the north. The perfume of the pines creates a heady mix with the sea breezes.

2 Circular Design
The round shape of the main structure is unique among Spanish castles and an example of 14th-century military architecture. The circular structure also aided in the collection of rainwater into the central cistern.

3 Defence Towers
The castle has three horseshoe-shaped towers and four smaller protuberances that were used for guard posts. Their windows have narrow slits, so that archers could attack without fear.

4 Keep Tower
The freestanding castle keep tower, called the Torre de Homenaje, is almost twice as high as the castle itself. The tower is connected to the roof by a small bridge supported by a slim and pointed Gothic archway.

5 Castle Ditch
In case the castle's thick walls and projecting turrets were insufficient deterrents for attackers, Mallorcan kings also surrounded the castle with an earthen ditch. The drawbridge would be lifted in during a siege.

TOP TIP

Reach Bellver hill yourself, or take the Hop-On Hop-Off bus, which stops at the castle.

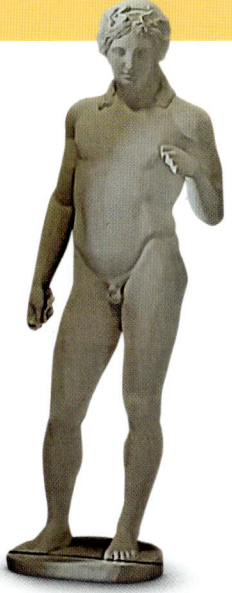

Clockwise from right
**Two-tiered arches of
the central courtyard;
ceramic vases on dis
play at the ground-
floor museum; Roman
statue at the first-
floor museum**

**6 Central
Courtyard**
The two-tiered central
courtyard has 21 Catalan
Romanesque arches on
the lower tier and 42
octagonal columns
supporting 21 Gothic
arches on the upper tier.
Statues of Venus and
Nero grace the walkway.

7 Hermaphroditus
The museum's star
exhibit is an alabaster

statue of the Greek god
Hermaphroditus, whose
body merged with a
nymph when he rejected
her advances. The dishev-
elled appearance is due
to a troubled sleep.

**8 Museum:
Ground Floor**
A museum on the history
of Palma surrounds the
central courtyard. Dis-
plays and exhibits on the
ground floor trace the
story of the city from its
Roman beginnings in 123
BCE to the present day.

**9 Museum:
First Floor**
This museum displays a
range of Roman statues,
busts and effigies that
were collected by 18th-
century antiquarian
Cardinal Antonio Despuig.

**Castell de Bellver,
overlooking the bay**

They were originally
on show at Raixa (p104).

10 Prison
Until 1915, the
lower reaches of this
castle were used as a
prison, dubbed La Olla
(the pot). Jaume III's
widow and sons were
imprisoned here.

Castell de Bellver Site Plan

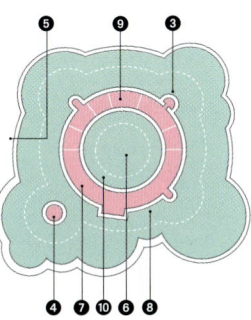

Key to Floorplan
🟩 Ground floor
🟥 First floor

FUNDACIÓ MIRÓ MALLORCA

⊙ C4 ⌂ C/Joan de Saridakis, 29, Palma ⊙ Hours vary, chech website
ⓦ miromallorca.com ↗

The artist Joan Miró lived and worked in Cala Major from 1956 until his death in 1983. Charting Miró's creative process and displaying various pieces, from oil on canvas to garden sculptures, this museum offers an intriguing insight into the artist's life and works. The building itself was the work of Rafael Moneo, a leading Spanish architect.

1 Works on Canvas

Many of these works from the 1960s and 1970s are made with mixed media – oil, chalk, acrylic and pastel. Some may have been inspired by Japanese Zen action painting. Some pieces are blue – for Miró, this was the most universal and optimistic colour – while other paintings are in black and white.

2 Temporary Exhibitions

The temporary exhibition spaces here feature the works of renowned international artists and also cover some of the lesser-known aspects of Miró's works, including paintings, drawings and sculptures.

3 Works on Paper

On display are several works on paper, most exhibiting the signature primary colours and bright splashes for which the artist is known.

4 Garden

In the garden, groups of rocks resembling water lilies "float" in a pool, while in other niches works by avant-garde and modern artists can be found. The peaceful surroundings are an ideal place to relax and reflect in.

5 Sculptures

Various vaguely anthropomorphic sculptures greet visitors in the garden, which functions as a gallery in itself. Downstairs, the giant *Woman and Bird* was made with ceramicist Llorens Artigas.

6 Son Boter

This 18th-century rural estate was Miró's second studio and the oldest of the Fundació's buildings. Some of the studio spaces still in use today, and workshops and courses by international artists are held at the nearby centre.

> **✂ EAT**
> The café in the sculpture garden has a superb terrace and offers free entry. It serves delicious sandwiches, *pa amb oli*, olives and fresh orange juice.

One of Miró's abstract paintings on canvas

Impressive design of the Fundació Miró Mallorca

7 Taller Sert

Designed by Josep Lluís Sert, Miró's studio looks like the artist just stepped out for a break from work in progress. The studio was designed to suit Miro's lifestyle as an artist. Objects that inspired Miró are all around: Hopi *kachina* dolls, a bat skeleton, Mexican terracottas and other everyday items.

8 Murals

Above one of the garden pools, a black rectangle encloses a ceramic mural by Miró, with colourful shapes gyrating in space. Taking up a whole wall in the café is a large mural of the sun and other celestial bodies.

9 Building Design

Composed of concrete made to look like travertine marble, the starkly modern building is softened by reflecting pools and trees. Its narrow windows afford surprising views from the hilltop site. Huge refined alabaster panels are also used as translucent walls, softly lighting exhibition spaces.

10 Mural del Sol

Usually on display is this five-panel sketch on paper, which formed the study for a mural commissioned for the UNESCO building in Paris, co-created with Llorens Artigas in 1955–8. The work won the Guggenheim award.

Fundació Miró Mallorca Site Plan

MIRÓ'S UNIQUE STYLE

Joan Miró (1893–1983), one of the best-known artists of the 20th century, was a Catalan through and through. Initially influenced by Fauvism, and later by Dadaism and Surrealism, he developed his own unique style, marked by lyricism and lively colouring. In Mallorca he became interested in graphics, ceramics and sculpture, scoring successes in every art form. Through his unique Catalan way of seeing the world, he became one of the greatest exponents of Surrealism.

CABRERA MARITIME NATIONAL PARK

📍 H6 🏛 Port of Cabrera; 971 176501

Designated a National Park in 1991, Spain's least-visited national park is an unspoiled haven of 90,000 hectares (224,000 acres) located just 18 km (11 miles) from Mallorca. The park is comprised of 19 islets, of which Cabrera ("goat island") is the only visitable island. This rocky island has spectacular coastlines and beaches, and its protected status has allowed bird and marine life to flourish.

Viewing platform at the castle

1 El Castell

Dating back to the 14th century, this clifftop fortification was built to defend against pirate attacks. The castle has since served as a hospital, a priest's residence and, famously, a prison for French soldiers during the Napoleonic Wars, who reportedly resorted to cannibalism due to the lack of resources.

2 El Far de N'Ensiolae

Sporting a distinctive red and white pattern, this 21-m- (68-ft-) tall lighthouse crowns the southernmost point of Cabrera and has been guiding ships since August 1870. Today, it's accessible via a trek that is fairly challenging but rewards visitors with sweeping sea views.

3 Sa Cova Blava

Only accessible by boat, the 20-m- (66-ft-) high Sa Cova Blava (the Blue Cave) is a natural wonder famous for its strikingly vivid blue waters. Visit in the afternoon to see how the cave got its name: its orientation means the afternoon sun reflects off the water and illuminates the cave's interior with an ethereal blue light.

4 Cabrera Museum

Occupying a 19th-century winery in the centre of Cabrera, this museum gives visitors a look at its natural history and heritage. Exhibits cover Punic and Roman archaeological remains, the island's ethnography and its unique flora and fauna.

🍴 EAT
There's only one eatery on the island: Sa Cantina, located next to the castle. It serves a tasty tapas-based menu and prices are reasonable.

Boats anchored in a bay on Cabrera

5 Botanical Garden

Just outside the Cabrera Museum, these small botanical gardens showcase the island's diverse flora and fauna with a focus on endemic species and conservation efforts. The island has over 400 botanical species, examples of which include rubia, Balearic buckthorn and dead horse arum lily.

6 Na Foradada

The most northern of Cabrera's islets, Na Foradada is a tiny island with a striking rock formation and lighthouse that have made it a popular subject for photographers. Though you'll spot a keeper's cottage next to the lighthouse, it was primarily maintained by the keepers at N'Ensiola.

7 Bird-watching

Bring your binoculars: this is a bird-watchers' paradise. There are over 120 species here, including Eleonora's falcons and Balearic warblers. Keep an eye out for rare and migratory birds, too, especially during spring and autumn.

8 Hiking

From coastal paths with sweeping views to inland routes over barren terrain, Cabrera offers a variety of hiking trails. There are routes for all abilities, but one of the most popular (and challenging) is an ascent to Vèrtex Picamosques, the island's highest point.

9 Snorkelling

Around 85 per cent of the park is underwater and, as a protected

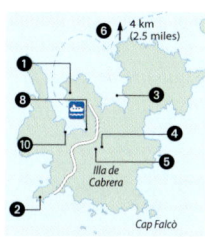

reserve, these are some of the most biodiverse waters in the Mediterranean, teeming with endemic fauna and marine life. If you're really lucky, you might even spot a loggerhead turtle or dolphin.

10 Beaches

Cabrera has an array of pristine sand, pebble and shingle beaches. Stick close to the port and visit the beautiful Sa Plageta and S'Espalmador beaches, where your main companions might be local lizards, or find one of the many hidden *calas* (coves) across Cabrera.

> **TOP TIP**
>
> Cabrera is a protected park with restrictions on visitor numbers, so book in advance.

VALLDEMOSSA

◪ C3

This small, picturesque town in the mountains is arguably where Mallorcan tourism began, in 1838, when composer Frédéric Chopin and his lover, the writer George Sand, rented rooms at the former monastery. Shunned by locals, the couple had a miserable time, as portrayed in Sand's book *A Winter in Majorca*. However, Mallorcans today are proud of their Chopin-Sand connection, and the book is sold everywhere.

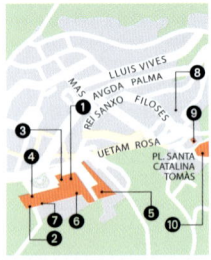

1 Monastery Complex

⊙ 10am–5pm Mon–Fri, 11am–4pm Sun ⓦ car toixadevalldemossa. com ◪

The town's top attraction is the former monastery where Chopin and Sand stayed, now home to a palace and a municipal museum *(p34)*. Given to the Carthusian Order in 1399, the estate was a monastery until 1835, when religious orders were ousted from the island. It was bought by a banker, who rented the rooms to Chopin.

2 Monastery: Prior's Cell

Second only to the abbot, the prior had a private oratory, a magnificent library, an elegant audience chamber, a bedroom, a dining room, an Ave María (praying alcove) and, of course, a sumptuous garden.

3 Monastery: Pharmacy

Laden with tinctures and various mysterious elixirs, a deconsecrated chapel faithfully re-creates the estate's original pharmacy. George Sand bought marshmallow here in a futile attempt to cure Chopin's tuberculosis.

4 Monastery: Church

The Neo-Classical church has a cupola adorned with frescoes by Fray Manuel Bayeu, Francisco de Goya's brother-in-law. It is distinguished by barrel vaulting and gilt-edged stucco work.

5 Monastery: Palace

The monastery's core was once the site of a palace built by Jaume II for his son. The rooms are regally decorated – a beautiful piece is the 12th-century wood-carving of Madonna and Child. Concerts of Chopin's music are also held in the Charterhouse of the palace.

6 Monastery: Cloisters

From the church, visitors can enter the cloisters known as the Myrtle Court. Around it are six chapels and ten spacious monks' cells. The International Chopin Festival is held here annually.

Ceiling fresco in the monastery church

Valldemossa's picturesque Old Town

TOP TIP

Roads in the town centre are for permit holders only. Park in one of the three car parks.

7 Monastery: Celda Chopin

🕙 10am–5.30pm daily 🔁

Said to be the room that Chopin and Sand rented, the cell is full of memorabilia, including Chopin's piano, Sand's manuscripts, busts and portraits.

8 Old Town

The Old Town spills down a hillside, surrounded by farmed terraces and *marjades* (stone walls) created 1,000 years ago by the Moors. The name "Valldemossa" comes from the original landowner, Muza. Many of the charming shops found here sell artisan goods, ideal for gifts.

9 Birthplace of Santa Catalina Thomás

Mallorca's only saint, Catalina Thomás (known as the "Beatata" for both her diminutive stature and saintliness), was born at a house on C/ Rectoría, 5 in 1531. The house was converted into an oratory in 1792 and features saintly scenes and a statue of her holding a bird. She was finally canonized in 1930 and many locals honour her with plaques by their doors.

10 Church of Sant Bartomeu

Near the bottom of the Old Town, a rustic, Baroque-style church is dedicated to one of the patron saints of Valldemossa. It was erected in 1245, which was shortly after Jaume I conquered Mallorca, and extended in the early 18th century. The striking bell tower and façade were added after 1863.

Frédéric Chopin's bust in the Celda Chopin room

Museu Municipal de Valldemossa

1. Archduke Luis Salvador of Habsburg-Lorena and Bourbon

On the ground floor here is a room dedicated to Archduke Luis Salvador, an indefatigable chronicler of Mediterranean life, whose absolute passion was Mallorcan culture. His nine volumes on the Balearics are the most exhaustive study ever made of the archipelago.

2. Mallorcan Painters of the Tramuntana

Mallorca's mountainous Tramuntana region has long attracted the skills of landscape painters. Among the outstanding artists shown are Bartomeu Ferrà, Joan Fuster and Antoni Ribas.

3. Catalan and Spanish Painters of the Tramuntana

Works by Sebastià Junyer, and more Impressionistic pieces by Eliseo Meifrén, are displayed here.

4. Guasp Printworks

On the ground floor of the museum visitors will also find a 17th-century hand press and one of the finest collections of intricate boxwood engravings in Europe. On the walls are prints executed on the press, which is still in working order.

The Guasp printwork press machine

5. International Painters of the Tramuntana

These include the 21st-century Italian master Aligi Sassu, whose works owe to Futurism, Surrealism and Expressionism.

6. Contemporary Art: Juli Ramis

The contemporary collection was conceived as a spotlight on Juli Ramis (1909–90), an important 20th-century Mallorcan painters. Works include his signature Dama Blava and pieces by his Paris contemporaries, showing a cross-fertilization of influences.

7. Miró

Of note is El Vol de l'Alosa (Flight of the Swallows) – Miró's whimsical illustrations for the works of Mallorcan poets in his signature bold and colourful style.

8. Picasso

Pablo Picasso, a lifelong friend of Miró and a frequent visitor to the area, is also represented in the museum's collection. There are several of his paintings of bulls and bullfighters, as well as some fine examples of book illustrations.

9. Tàpies

Also in the last room are a few works by another great Catalan painter, Antoni Tàpies. Master of an elegant and totally unique artistic style, he created works that have little in common with the more Surrealist images of his compatriots Miró and Dalí, and are considerably more understated, poetic and monumental.

10. Other 20th-Century Artists

Finally, there is a collection of some small but significant engravings and lithographs by great modern artists from around the world, including German Surrealist Max Ernst, Italian Futurist Robert Matta, French Dadaist André Masson, the English master Henry Moore and British-Irish painter Francis Bacon.

FROM MASS TOURISM TO CULTURE AND ECOLOGY

Once an isolated backwater and the largest of the Balearic Islands, Mallorca became known for all the wrong reasons after the French Romantic writer, George Sand shared an account of her disastrous trip with Frédéric Chopin in her autobiographical travel novel A Winter in Majorca. By the early 20th century, however, the famous French novelist and poet, Jules Verne visited the islands and was inspired by its magnificent caves and the Kaiser Wilhelm II ship was cruising its waters. In the 1960s, the island turned its attention towards mass tourism with rapid development that resulted in the construction and functioning of scores of high-rise hotels, restaurants and cafés. This tourism boom significantly boosted the economy of Mallorca, but also started having severe impacts on the environment and culture of the island. Since the early 21st century, a much greater emphasis has been placed on saving the island's culture and ecology. Necessary steps have been taken such as nature parks have been created, salt pans saved, the black vulture spared from extinction, and inland and rural buildings have been protected as part of the island's heritage.

Lily pond at the Jardí Botànic de Sóller

SÓLLER VALLEY

📍 C2

Famous for its orange and lemon groves, Sóller, an enchanting town embraced by the Tramuntana mountains on the northwest coast, is often referred to as the heart of the Golden Valley. During the late 19th and early 20th centuries, many locals traded oranges, olive oil and textiles through Sóller's port. The neighbouring villages of Fornalutx and Biniaraix can be reached on foot from the Plaça de Constitució.

Balearic Museum of Natural Sciences

1 Historic Train and Tram

The historic train travels through pretty mountain scenery on its hour-long journey from Palma to Sóller. A vintage tram trundles through orange groves between Sóller and the port.

2 Port de Sóller

The picturesque port area (p103) offers many restaurants, sandy beaches and fabulous views. A steep walk up leads to Oratorio de Santa Caterina, built in 1280. The Jumeirah Luxury Spa & Hotel is also worth a visit.

3 Balearic Museum of Natural Sciences

📍 C2 🏠 Ctra. Palma, km 30 ⏰ 10am–2pm Mon–Sat 🌐 museuciencies naturals.org 🔗

Set in an old palace, this museum holds a great collection dedicated to the study of nature and conservation in the Balearic Islands. See the library and classroom,

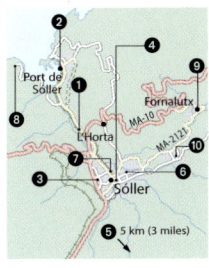

and the lovely botanical gardens nearby.

4 Plaça de Constitució

Sóller's main square is ideal for people-watching. Directly on the *plaça* stands the sandstone church of Sant Bartomeu, parts of which date from the 1100s. Nearby is the pretty Art Nouveau Bank of Sóller, built in 1912.

5 Jardins d'Alfàbia

A legacy of the Moorish talent for landscaping and irrigation, these gardens *(p50)* date to the 13th century. There is

also a lavish country home here, which is worth exploring.

6 Can Prunera Art Museum

⏰ 10:30am–6pm Tue–Sat

Set in an Art Nouveau building, with period furniture and fittings, this museum exhibits work by 19th- and 20th-century artists.

7 Fet a Sóller

Head to Fet a Sóller *(p107)*, next to the market square, where traditional ice cream is made and sold. You can choose from 40 delicious flavours and sorbets all made from natural ingredients. There

---

☕ **DRINK**
The garden snack bar at Jardins d'Alfàbia offers fresh juices along with nuts, fruits and snacks, all produced at its working farm.

Towering Cap de Gros Lighthouse

is also a café and a small gift shop for souvenirs.

8 Cap de Gros Lighthouse

It is worth the steep walk up the mountain road to the landmark Cap de Gros lighthouse above Sóller port. Although it was built in 1842, it was not fitted with electricity until 1918. The views across the bay are magnificent.

9 Fornalutx Village

This labyrinthine village *(p102)* in the Tramuntanas is a pleasant walk from the main square. A traditional settlement, it has stunning mountain views, a small square and a 17th-century church.

10 Biniaraix Village

This village *(p106)* comes alive in the holiday season and on weekends, when walkers flock to its cobbled Barranc steps. These lead to the Cuber reservoir and L'Ofre, one of the Tramuntanas' highest peaks.

Seaside setting of Port de Sóller

SANTUARI DE LLUC

D2 **Plaza Peregrins 1, Lluc** **lluc.net**

The monastery at Lluc is the spiritual centre of Mallorca and has been a place of pilgrimage for over 800 years. The main point of interest is the little statue of the Virgin (La Moreneta). The story goes that it was found by a local shepherd boy who showed it to the nearest monk. The image was initially moved to the church but it kept returning to the same spot, so a chapel was built to house it. Each year, thousands of pilgrims come to pay homage.

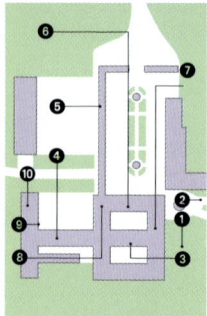

Santuari de Lluc Site Plan

1 The Complex

The complex is rather plain but is set in fragrant forests of pine and holm oak, and laid out around courtyards. There is a good hostel, a choir school, several restaurants, campsites, picnic facilities and a covered area for outdoor celebrations and services.

2 El Camí dels Misteris del Rosari

"The Way of the Mysteries of the Rosary" is a pilgrim route up the hill behind the complex, where a crucifix awaits. The path is punctuated by bronze sculptures framed in stone.

3 Basilica Entrance

The façade of the church, facing an inner courtyard is an appealing Baroque confection that relieves the plainness of the surrounding structures. The bronze statue here is that of a bishop who helped to renovate the place in the early 1900s.

4 Basilica Interior

The Renaissance-style church was deemed a Minor Basilica in 1962 by Pope John XXIII – its

 EAT
Head to Sa Fonda, for Mallorcan fare, or Restaurant Ca S'Amitger *(casa mitger.es)* for roast lamb, goat and rice *brut*, a Mallorcan country dish.

great embellishments are probably the reason. Spectacular crystal chandeliers light the way, and the beautiful gold altarpiece is alive with figures.

Santuari de Lluc complex amid verdant forest

Interior of the basilica

5 Els Porxets
The gallery of the old pilgrim's hospice is a picturesque arcaded corridor, with ground-floor stables and bedrooms off the passageway on the upper level. Declared a Spanish Historical Artistic Monument, it has been carefully restored.

6 Museum: Religious Artifacts
Pieces on display include a Byzantine *trikerion* (three-part sacred utensil), a 15th-century wooden tabernacle, a Flemish Virgin and Child, a gold filigree reliquary for a Piece of the True Cross, and paintings.

7 Museum: Majolica
In the 15th century, Italy imported large amounts of tin-glazed pottery from Spain by way of the trade route through Mallorca, hence the term "majolica", from the medieval name of the island. Until the early 20th century, this type of pottery was also produced in Mallorca.

8 Museu de Lluc
🕐 10am–6pm daily
A broad collection of Mallorcana includes fascinating prehistoric and ancient artifacts, coins, religious treasures, vestments, sculptures, ceramics and paintings, as well as models of Mallorcan rooms from the 17th century.

9 La Moreneta
In a special chapel stands the object of pilgrimage, La Moreneta ("the Little Dark One") – or, to be more precise, a mid-13th-century, possibly Flemish, version of her. To some, the lighting added in the 1960s seems incongruous with the rest of the chapel.

10 Els Blauets
The 50-boy choir Els Blauets (The Blues) was established in 1531, and is named after their blue cassocks worn during celebrations. They sing in the afternoon at 1:15pm from Monday to Friday.

Els Blauets Choir boys

PENÍNSULA DE FORMENTOR

📍 F1

The final jutting spur of the Serra de Tramuntana mountain range has stunning views, sandy beaches and the island's first luxury resort. With weird rock formations and jagged edges pointing up at 45 degrees, its mountains rise to over 330 m (1,000 ft). The peninsula can be reached by car from nearby Port de Pollença; it's a beautiful stretch, though take care of tight bends.

1 Peninsula Road
The famous winding coastal road is narrow but well maintained, forking off to the Four Seasons Resort in one direction and across to the cape in the other. Side roads along the way – some of which are not well maintained – wind up to the watchtower and give access to the beach, as well as makeshift car parks for Cala Figuera.

2 Flora and Fauna
The peninsula is a wild landscape of pine trees, scrub, clump grasses, cactus and plenty more. On a hot summer's day, with cicadas buzzing, walkers will likely see goats, lizards and birds.

3 Talaia d'Albercutx
This watchtower has an amazing view over the peninsula and bays of Pollença and Alcúdia. The road to it is rough and a four-wheel-drive car is recommended. To reach the top, hike the last bit and climb the tower itself.

TOP TIP

From June to September, private vehicles are restricted from entering the peninsula.

Mountain goats on the rocky terrain

Admiring the Península de Formentor

7 Casas Velles
An old Mallorcan house is preserved in the grounds of the Hotel Formentor. There is a characteristic courtyard with an old stone well, a one-room house and a small chapel complete with a melodramatic, life-size crucifix.

8 Mountain Tunnel
The road continues through pine woods and past more miradors on its way to Es Fumat mountain. It then tunnels through the raw rock of the mountain. For those who need more thrills, there is a steep staircase up the cliff above the tunnel's western mouth.

9 Cap de Formentor
Mallorca's northernmost peninsula is a good spot for a day-long excursion. The terrain becomes rockier towards the end of the peninsula, where the view plunges down to Cala Figuera,

Mallorca's most inaccessible beach. It is a challenging drive out to the end, but the breathtaking views are worth it.

10 Lighthouse
Around the last curve of the road leading to the northernmost tip of Mallorca, is this historic silver-domed lighthouse, set on a dramatic promontory with views out to sea. On a clear day, you can see all the way to Menorca.

> ☕ **DRINK**
> Inside the lighthouse, the Far Formentor café has snacks and drinks. Sit and relax on the broad terrace and enjoy the views.

4 Main Miradors
Of the main miradors (viewpoints), Mirador de Mal Pas is closest to the road. From here it is possible to walk along a wall with dizzying panoramas of the rocks and sea below.

5 Beach
Nestled in a long, sheltered cove with fine sand and clear turquoise water, the pretty Platja de Formentor is served both by road and a regular ferry from Port de Pollença. Eating spots and *tiki* shades abound. Expect crowds of families at weekends.

6 Four Seasons Resort Mallorca
🏠 C/de Formentor, s/n
🌐 fourseasons.com

This exclusive resort has been spoiling the rich and famous, such as Winston Churchill, Audrey Hepburn and Elizabeth Taylor, since 1929. In 2024 it reopened as a Four Seasons Resort after an extensive four-year redevelopment.

Brilliant blue waters at Cap Formentor

Calm waters off Platja de Formentor

ALCÚDIA

⊞ F2

Located at the base of a peninsula, this delightful walled town was originally a Phoenician settlement and the capital of the island under the Romans. It was later destroyed by the Vandals, then rebuilt by the Moors, and prospered as a trading centre well into the 19th century. Extensively restored, the town contains many sites of interest from its fascinating past.

1 Ca'n Torró Library
⌂ C/d'en Serra, 15
⊙ Hours vary, chech website ☒ cantorro.es

Opened in 1990, the library is housed in a 14th-century aristocratic building. It hosts concerts and exhibitions.

2 Oratori de Sant Ana
This tiny medieval chapel, on the main road to Port d'Alcúdia, was built in the 13th century and has a stone carving of a rather stocky Virgin and Child supported by an angel.

3 Ajuntament
The handsome Renaissance-style Town Hall was given its present look in 1929. Above the balcony is a grand tower with a clock, belfry and weather vane, its overhanging pitched roofs gaily tiled in red and green stripes.

4 Teatre Romà
⌂ C/de Sant Ana ⊠
The island's only intact Roman theatre is also Spain's smallest surviving example. Even so, it would have held about 2,000 people, and today is sometimes the venue for special concerts.

5 Pollentia Ruins
The Roman city reached its peak in the 1st and 2nd centuries CE, and the foundations of what may have been the forum and *insulae* (apartments) are visible. Many of the stones have been removed over the years.

6 Arab Quarter
The narrow streets of the Old Town are resonant of life under Moorish rule, long after Roman orderliness had disappeared. No one knows exactly where the old *souk* (market) was, but it is easy to imagine artisans' shops spilling onto the dusty streets.

7 City Walls
The walls were constructed after the Spanish reconquest of the island in the 14th century *(p9)*, with a second ring added in the 17th century. By the 19th century they had begun to show their age and the vagaries of expansion, but they have now been restored almost to their original state. They are adorned with gates and 26 towers in all.

8 Historic Centre
While modern Alcúdia extends beyond the old city walls and has a commercial port town attached to it, most of the sights of historic interest are located within or near the walls. These include churches, mansions, a museum and some of the island's most significant Roman ruins.

9 Beaches
From Alcúdia's main beach – the 7-km-(4-mile-) long stretch of the Platja Gran – to the secret coves of the Cap de Pinar, this beautiful stretch of Mallorca's northwestern coastline has a glorious choice of beaches and bays.

 EAT
There are lots of good places to eat in Port d'Alcúdia. Try the cafés along the waterfront or head to Como en Casa *(p119)*, which serves great salads and tapas.

Altar at the Sant Jaume Church

10 Sant Jaume Church
🏠 Plaça Jaume Quès
📞 971 548665 🕐 Hours vary, call ahead ♿
The 14th-century church collapsed in 1870 but was rebuilt. The rose window is lovely, and the inner recesses feature elaborate gold altars. There is also a museum displaying ancient artifacts.

The scenic resort town of Alcúdia

COVES DEL DRAC

📍 G4 🏠 Porto Cristo 🕐 Hours vary, check website 🌐 cuevasdeldrach.com ↗

These limestone caves were first mapped out by geologist Édouard Martel in 1896. They have since become one of Mallorca's top attractions. Hundreds of people at a time make their way along the cavernous path to see the artfully lit rock formations and lakes. The name "Drac" comes from the Catalan word for "dragon", probably in reference to the mythical creature's role as the fierce guardian of secret treasure.

1 Garden
As most visitors will have to wait a little before their tour begins, there is a thoughtfully created garden by the entrance. Mediterranean trees and plants, such as olives, figs, violets and hibiscus, provide the setting for striking displays of limestone – one piece even evokes the shape of a dragon. Gorgeous peacocks roam freely around the gardens, which make a lovely spot for a picnic.

2 Four Chambers
Visitors descend to the caves through the Luis Armand Chamber, part of the Frenchman's Cave, which was charted by Martel. The three other main caverns are called Black Cave, White Cave and Luis Salvador's Cave. The path is smooth and even, and the guides are temporarily silent, so that visitors can have the opportunity to contemplate the beauty of the place.

3 Subterranean Lakes
Lake Martel is one of the world's largest underground lakes, at 177 m (580 ft) long, with an average width of 30 m (98 ft). Its calm waters beautifully reflect the lighting effects.

4 Lighting
The illuminations in the caves are the work of light engineer Carlos Buigas. Crevices, planes, chasms and spaces are all highlighted in colours to maximize the effects of chiaroscuro and depth. The lighting was installed in 1935.

5 Formations
The stalactites (those hanging from above), stalagmites

(those below), and columns (where the two meet) range from the finest needles to monumental massifs. There are also deep ravines, at the bottom of which are impossibly turquoise pools.

6 The Snow-Capped Mountain Stalactite

It was Archduke Luis Salvador of Austria who commissioned a team of Frenchmen to investigate the caves. He loved studying the wonderful landscape of Mallorca and particularly the snow-capped mountain stalactite in the first chamber.

7 Fanciful Figures

Formations dubbed the "Inquisition Chamber" or "Ariadne's Labyrinth" were so named in the Middle Ages; the "Snowy Mount" and "Ruined

Boat ride inside the cave

Castle" speak of more modern imaginations.

8 Performances

Seated in a charming amphitheatre, the audience is regaled with a fascinating display at the end of the tour. Hypnotic lighting effects perfectly accompany live music from a quartet on a rowing boat. The main highlights include Albinoni's *Adagio*, Pachelbel's *Canon*, and serene works by Chopin, Handel, Boccherini, Bach and others. Photography is not permitted here.

9 Boat Ride

As a delightful climax to the sound-and-light performance, visitors are offered boat rides on the lake – eight to a boat – steered by skilled gondoliers who employ an elegant figure-of-eight rowing style.

10 Exit

Visitors exit the complex by foot, past the Lake of the Grand Duchess of Tuscany and Chamber of the Columns to the Vestibule, a funnel-like tunnel leading back up to the surface.

MALLORCA'S CAVES

The Coves del Drac and the Coves d'es Hams are the best known of Mallorca's cave systems, but there are many more. The stalagmites and stalactites of the Coves de Campanet and the Coves d'Artà (the latter also features a sound- and-light show) are quite impressive, while the Coves de Gènova are conveniently accessible from Palma, if a little less dramatic.

Stalactites in the cave

TOP 10 OF EVERYTHING

De La Soca bakery

HISTORIC PLACES

Mediterranean Sea

Cap de Formentor

Pollença ❻
Alcúdia ❹
Sóller
Tramuntana
Valldemossa
Inca Muro ❶
Serra de ❸ ❽ Alaró Artà ❾
Palma Manacor
Andratx ❺ ❷
Felanitx
Porto Cristo
Campos
❿
Santanyí
❼
Colònia de
Sant Jordi

0 km   20
0 miles   20

1 Necropolis at Son Real

Set on a glorious headland on the northern coast, this Talayotic necropolis (p113) dates back to the 7th century BCE. Most of the funerary objects discovered here were taken to Madrid, but some still remain on site in a small museum.

2 Banys Àrabs, Palma

These private baths (p95) probably belonged to a wealthy Moorish resident and, together with their gardens, have survived to this day virtually intact. However, closer examination reveals elements from even earlier sources. The columns, each one different, were doubtless taken from an ancient Roman building.

3 Jardins d'Alfàbia

C2 Ctra. Palma–Sóller, km 17
mid-Feb–Oct 9:30–6:30 daily
jardinesdealfabia.com

The origins of this majestic garden and house are lost to history, though it's believed to date back to Roman times. Although Renaissance and Baroque touches are evident, the underlying Moorish styling predominates. The many watercourses are distinctly Moorish, as well as the oasis-like groves of trees encircling pools, where you can sit and enjoy the fresh air and gurgling rivulets.

4 Pollentia

The Moorish town of Alcúdia is built over an ancient Roman settlement called Pollentia (p44). Little more than a few original Roman columns and foundations remain in situ – after being burned by Vandals in 440 CE, the antique structures were dismantled to help create the new town.

**Small chamber in the
Banys Àrabs, Palma**

5 Palau de l'Almudaina, Palma

Palma's old, rambling palace *(p95)* displays a mixture of Gothic and Moorish styles.

6 Castell del Rei

The Moors chose another picturesque spot for their "Castle of the King" *(p116)*. The ruins we see today are the remains of medieval embellishments made by Jaume I. The castle did not effectively defend against pirates, but it was the very last stronghold to surrender to Aragonese invasions in the 14th century. The interior is not open to the public.

7 Ses Covetes

Midway along the beach at Es Trénc is the site *(p124)* of what were probably ancient Roman burial grounds, where cinerary urns containing the ashes of the dead were placed in small niches. Known as a columbarium (from columba, Latin for dove), it resembles a pigeon house, with small openings lined up in rows.

8 Castell d'Alaró

This lofty castle *(p105)* was originally used by the Moors as a stronghold. It proved to be virtually

**Steps leading to the
Castell d'Alaró**

impregnable – conquered only after long sieges, with its defenders eventually being starved out. The Christians refurbished the structure and continued to use it for centuries.

9 Ses Païsses

These Bronze Age remains form one of Mallorca's most impressive prehistoric sites *(p121)*. The defensive wall, composed of square blocks, is an example of the Mediterranean Cyclopean style – so named by later cultures who believed that only a giant like the Cyclops could have built such a structure.

10 Capocorb Vell

These well-preserved megalithic ruins *(p123)* of the Talayotic culture that dominated the island some 3,000 years ago are similar to the ones found at Ses Païsses. The word "talayot" refers to the towers at such sites, which were usually two or three storeys high. The central round towers are the oldest elements here; an encircling wall and square towers complete the complex.

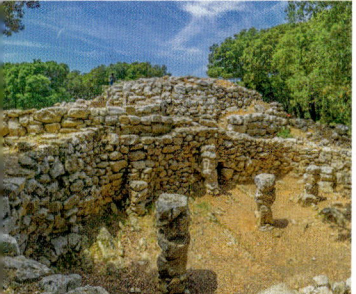

**Fragment of a defensive wall
at Ses Païsses**

MONASTERIES

Interior of the Carthusian Monastery, Valldemossa

Randa table mountain in the 13th century, and it was here that he trained missionaries bound for Africa and Asia. Nothing remains of the original building, but Llull's legacy has ensured that the site is an important place for many Catholics. The monastery houses a library and study centre, and visitors are welcome to stay overnight in simple rooms. There are other hermitages lower down the hill.

1 Carthusian Monastery, Valldemossa

Set in one of the most appealing towns (p32) on the island, this former monastery and royal residence has a rich history. Most captivating of all to its myriad visitors is the poignant story of the winter visit of Polish composer Frédéric Chopin, sick with tuberculosis, and his lover George Sand, along with her two children.

2 Ermita de Sant Miquel
📍 E4

Just east of Montuïri is a small monastery with views over the fertile fields of Es Pla. Facilities include a café-restaurant and nicely restored monks' cells, where, for a nominal amount, visitors can stay, as long as they do not mind sharing a bathroom with other guests.

3 Santuari de Nostra Senyora de Cura
📍 E4

Ramon Llull (p91) founded this hermitage at the top of the Puig de

4 Santuari de Nostra Senyora de Gràcia
📍 E4

The lowest hermitage site on Puig de Randa is set on a ledge in a cliff above a sheer 200-m (656-ft) drop and has great views out over the plain. It was founded in 1497 and appears, along with nesting birds, to be sheltered by the huge rock that overhangs it.

5 Ermita de Sant Llorenç
📍 D2

At Cala Tuent on the island's wild and less built-up northern coast is a small 13th-century hermitage perched high above the sea. It was built in a remote location and remains relatively isolated from Mallorca's crowds to this day.

6 Ermita de Nostra Senyora de Bonany
📍 F4

This monastery is perched on top of Puig de Bonany. A stone cross was erected here in 1749 for Junípero Serra (p129), before he left on a mission to California. The sanctuary was built in the 17th century as an act of thanks-giving for a good harvest – *bon any* or "good year". The modern church dates from 1925 and is entered via an imposing gate decorated with ceramic portraits of St Paul and St Anthony. The forecourt has panoramic views.

Santuari de Sant Salvador looming over Artà

7 Santuari de Lluc

Not so much an active monastery as a place of pilgrimage that also draws tourists, this is Mallorca's holiest spot *(p38)* and has been a sacred zone since time immemorial. Set high in the mountains, the complex has an attractive church, with a special chapel to house the venerated image of the Virgin Mary. There are plenty of pilgrim paths to climb and beautiful nature trails to explore.

8 Santuari de la Mare de Déu del Puig

Just to the south of Pollença, this serene place *(p115)* with marvellous views houses one of the oldest Gothic images of the Virgin on the island. The unassuming complex, dating mostly from the 1700s, comprises a courtyard, a chapel, fortified walls, a refectory and simple rooms. The latter can also be rented for an overnight stay.

9 Ermita de Betlem
G3

Up in the hills northwest of Artà *(p122)*, this monastery has a lovely vantage point, 400 m (1,312 ft) above the sea. It dates from 1804, when a group of hermits decided to rebuild the church that had been destroyed years before

by pirates. The church is tiny, but it is worth the detour. The surrounding area has good spots for a picnic.

10 Santuari de Sant Salvador

Built in 1348, the Santuari de Sant Salvador *(p123)* was sought as a protected place from the Black Death plague. Pilgrims and other visitors can stay overnight at this former monastery, which has a truly spectacular setting, right at the top of the picturesque Serres de Llevant mountains. It is difficult to miss: the site's huge stone cross and statue of Christ can be seen for miles around.

CHURCHES

1 Sant Bernat, Petra

Petra *(p129)* was the birthplace of Fray Junípero Serra, who established Catholic missions all over California in the 1700s and early 1800s. The town's stocky church, Sant Bernat, commemorates the man.

2 Parròquia de Santa Maria de Sineu, Sineu

Mallorca's grandest parish church stands at the highest point of a town *(p130)* that was declared the official centre of the island by King Sanç. It has a small archaeological museum (open only on Wednesday).

3 Església de Santa Eulàlia, Palma

Built just after the Christians reclaimed the Balearics in the 13th century and dedicated to Eulalia, the patron saint of Barcelona, this old church *(p98)* has a rare Gothic homogeneity, despite some later medieval touches and a few 19th-century additions.

4 Oratori de Montesió, Porreres

◙ E4

Part of a former monastery, this 14th-century hilltop church overlooks the small agricultural village of Porreres. It has a five-sided cloister, an unusual arcaded façade with elegant Gothic lines, and great views out to sea. The setting makes a wonderful venue for special concerts sponsored by the town, featuring internationally known talents.

5 Nostra Senyora de la Esperança, Capdepera

The story goes that once, when a band of loutish brigands were preparing to attack Capdepera *(p121)*, the townspeople implored the Madonna to help them. A thick fog promptly settled in, confounding the pirates. Since then, the town's statue has been known as Sa Esperança ("the bringer of hope"). It is housed in a Gothic chapel within the famous castle at Capdepera.

Nostra Senyora de la Esperança, Capdepera

6 La Seu, Palma

Mallorca's cathedral, La Seu (*p22*) is the most precious architectural treasure of the Balearic Islands and is regarded as one of Spain's most outstanding Gothic structures. Its imposing exterior, complete with flamboyant spires, leads into a vast space full of treasures, including one of the world's largest stained-glass windows. An integral part of the cathedral is its museum, which stores precious works of religious art.

7 Santuari Ermita de la Victòria

The fortress church (*p116*) was built on a rocky headland near Alcúdia in the 1600s to house an early statue of the Virgin. Despite these measures, this figure was stolen twice by pirates. The church makes a great starting point for hikes over the promontory.

8 Basílica de Sant Francesc, Palma

Built in 1281 on a site where the Moors made soap, this church (*p96*) has suffered its share of woes, most notably when struck by lightning in 1580. Consequently, the façade you see today is a Baroque creation, though presumably no less massive than the original Gothic structure. The beautiful cloisters are the star turn, and, in fact, you must go through them first to enter the church.

9 Portals Vells Cave Church

📍 B5

One of the caves along the rocky headland of Portals Vells has been turned into a church, Cova de la Mare de Déu. According to legend, shipwrecked Genoese sailors who were grateful for their survival began worshipping here. The holy water stoup and altar have been carved out of solid rock, although the effigy of the Virgin that was once here is now in a seafront church at Portals Nous.

Altar at Nostra Senyora dels Àngels, Pollença

10 Nostra Senyora dels Àngels, Pollença

Built in a Baroque style, this parish church has Greek-Roman features including a rose window with elaborate stone tracery outside, and an intriguing sculpture, located in a side chapel, of St Sebastian nonchalantly resting on the arrows that pierce his body. Note the floor tiles beautifully decorated with cockerel heads, the symbol of the town of Pollença (*p114*).

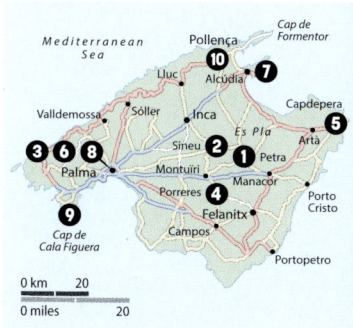

CASTLES AND TOWERS

Arcades surrounding the courtyard, Castell de Bellver

1 Castell de Bellver

One of just a handful of round castles (p26) in the world, and impeccably preserved, this building conjures up fairy-tale images of sensational adventures. In fact, its history is a little more prosaic – it was built as a summer residence for Jaume II in the early 14th century and later used as a prison for enemies of the Crown for hundreds of years. It has a great collection of classical sculptures and the views over the Bay of Palma are spectacular.

2 Sant Joan Baptista Belfry

🗺 E3

Located in the traditional rural town of Muro (p130), this beautiful bell tower seems almost Moorish, so slender is the arch that joins it to the imposing church. However, it sports other elements that recall Gothic and Renaissance styles, including stone carvings, a decorative door and coffers. It is situated in one of the island's prettiest squares.

3 Castell d'Alaró

This remote castle (p105), found high in the hills on the island's north-west side, was attacked several times over the centuries, each time proving its defences against everything but prolonged siege. Alfonso III, on his invasion of the island, finally took it in 1285. The leaders of the patriots were burned alive by the king, who, in turn, was excommunicated by the Pope.

4 Castell del Rei

With Moorish origins and Christian additions, this castle (p116) never served its defensive purpose well, as raiders simply avoided it. It was demoted to a watchtower, and, in the early 18th century, abandoned altogether. Today, it is a panoramic destination for hikers.

5 Tower on Illa Dragonera

The ancient watchtower on one of Mallorca's most picturesque island nature reserves (p106) may date as far back as Roman times. It might not be much to look at these days, but it's fun just to hike around the unspoiled island and imagine what it must have been like during a raid, with corsairs storming the place and signal fires warning the rest of the island.

6 Talaia d'Albercutx

At the highest point on the Península de Formentor (p40) is a tower that is notable for having been built at all in such a precipitous place. At this height, the wind howls, and the views down below are like those from a helicopter.

7 Castell de Cabrera

🗺 H6 🕐 Daily

The 14th-century castle on the island of Cabrera, off Mallorca's south coast, has a chequered history, subsequent to its original purpose as a defence measure for the southern reaches of the main island. At various times it has been a pirates' den; a crowded, deadly prison for 9,000 French soldiers in the 19th century; and an outpost for General Franco's Fascist forces in the 20th century. Now the island it oversees is a national park, and stupendous views reward those who climb up to the crumbling fortress.

8 Castell de Santueri
F5 Cami des Castell, Felanitx Apr–Sep: 10:30am–6pm daily

One of several castles with the same name, this one is about 6 km (4 miles) southeast of Felanitx. It was built in the 14th century on the site of a ruined Arab fortress and is set on a plateau of a mountain in the Serra de Llevant. The view here stretches from the Cap de Formentor to Cabrera.

9 Torre des Verger
B3

Found at the Mirador de Ses Ànimes, this watchtower, built in 1579, provides what must be among the finest views of the entire western coastline. Visitors can climb up into the stone structure

and stand on the topmost level, just as watchmen must have done in the 16th and 17th centuries when Mallorca came under almost incessant attack by North African brigands.

10 Castell de Capdepera
This is another Mallorcan fortress that epitomizes the fairy-tale castle. The approach is a pleasure in itself, as you pass fragrant plants and rocky outcrops, and the views of the surrounding town (p121) are memorable. It was built by King Sanç in the 14th century.

Enjoying the view from the Torre des Verger

MODERNISTA BUILDINGS IN PALMA

1 Can Forteza Rey
📍 N3 🏠 Plaça del Marquès del Palmer, 1

Local architect Lluís Forteza Rey designed this splendid five-storey apartment building, which is richly decorated in sculptures and *trencadís* (a mosaic of broken tiles). Antoni Gaudí, then working at the cathedral alongside Forteza's father, is said to have contributed ideas for its design.

2 Edificio Paraires
📍 M4 🏠 Corner of C/Paraires and C/Minyones

The work of local architect Francesc Roca i Simó, this three-storey building features his characteristically refined and restrained style. The most notable features are the large curved windows on each floor, which are decorated with elegant wrought ironwork.

3 Can Roca
📍 M3 🏠 C/Sant Nicolau, 18

One of the first Modernista buildings in Palma to use ceramic decoration on its façade, this edifice dates from the turn of the 20th century and is also the work of Francesc Roca i Simó.

4 Parlament (Antiguo Círculo Mallorquín)
📍 M4 🏠 C/Conquistador, 11 📞 971 228281 🕐 9am–1pm Mon–Fri

The Mallorcan parliament occupies a building that was both a casino and

Historic Can Forteza Rey apartment building

a cultural centre in the 19th century. A 1913 expansion gave it the elegant Modernista façade visible today. It is advisable to book your visit in advance.

5 Forn des Teatre
N3 Plaça de Weyler, 9
9am–8pm Mon–Sat
fornetdelasoca.com

Modernista architects didn't just design mansions and hotels. The shops also adopted the style, exemplified by this bakery. Although the original shop closed, the current owner has retained the Modernista façade, with swirling woodwork, painted panels crowned by a dragon and an iconic sign. The bakery is now called Fornet de la Soca.

6 Gran Hotel
N3 Plaça de Weyler, 3
10am–8pm daily caixaforum. es/palma

This famous Modernista mansion was designed by famed architect Lluís Domènech i Montaner, and now houses the CaixaForum. It features undulating balconies, tile decoration and an exuberant use of floral motifs. Monthly tours are available but must be pre-booked.

7 Almacenes El Águila
N3 Plaça del Marquès del Palmer, 1

Designed in 1908 by Gaspar Bennàssar and Jaume Alenyà, this former department store made use of novel construction techniques and materials. Iron columns allowed for the incorporation of vast windows that let natural light flood in. The building also has a lavish façade.

8 Can Casasayas and Pension Menorquina
M3 Plaça del Mercat

Gaudí's influence is apparent in this charming pair of Art Nouveau-style buildings (designed by Francesc Roca i Simó), which exhibit his trademark parabolic arches and swooping curves. Plans to connect the two buildings – separated only by a narrow street – were not approved by the city council.

9 Casa de las Medias
N4 C/Colom, 11

This curious building is covered with the colourful broken tile decoration popularized by the Modernistas. Its name, which means "the house of stockings", comes from the haberdashery that once occupied the ground floor. The five-storey building has unusual pyramid-shaped balconies.

10 Can Corbella
M4 Plaça de Cort, 1

The impressive Can Corbella is situated in the heart of Palma in Plaça de Cort. Its striking horseshoe arches at the entrance illustrate the Neo-Mudéjar style popular in the late 19th century, and is seen as a precursor to the Modernista movement.

Decorative Can Corbella at the corner of Plaça de Cort

MUSEUMS

Inside the the Museu Fundación Juan March, Palma

1 Museu Fundación Juan March, Palma

A 17th-century mansion *(p98)*, once the headquarters of the family-owned Banca March, was one of the finer legacies left by founder and Mallorcan financier Juan March. It now houses an extensive exhibition of contemporary Spanish art, including works by Picasso, Miró, Dalí, and Mallorca's greatest living painter, Miquel Barceló.

Clay pots at Museu Monogràfic, Alcúdia

2 Museu de Lluc

This museum *(p39)* contains an interesting hotchpotch of pre-historic artifacts, Roman finds, ceramics, religious pieces, and an exhaustive array of works by 20th-century Valldemossan artist Josep Coll Bardolet, who was known for his boldly coloured landscapes.

3 Museu Municipal de Valldemossa

The range of objects on display here *(p34)* is vast and eclectic, covering the history of printing in Mallorca, the work of an Austrian archduke, paintings inspired by the mountains of the Tramuntana, and important works by modern masters.

4 Es Baluard, Palma

🗺 J4 🏠 Plaça Porta de Santa Catalina 10 🕐 10am–8pm Tue–Sat, 10am–3pm Sun 🌐 esbaluard.org 🗘

A 16th-century fortress on the waterfront now houses Palma's excellent contemporary art museum. The permanent collection has works by Dalí, Miró and Tàpies among others, and the temporary exhibitions are always interesting.

5 Fundació Miró Mallorca, Palma

Miró had connections to Mallorca; both his mother and his wife were Mallorcan-born, and the great artist spent the last 27 years of his life here. His studio during that final period has been turned into a museum *(p28)* devoted to his work.

6 Museu Monogràfic, Alcúdia

🗺 F2 🏠 C/Sant Jaume, 30 📞 971 547004 🕐 9:30am–2:30pm Tue–Sat 🗘

This small but beautifully designed museum houses all the finds from ancient Roman Pollentia, such

8 Museu d'Art Sacre de Mallorca, Palma

Housed in the former Episcopal Palace, this treasure trove *(p97)* contains numerous archaeological artifacts, ceramics, coins, books and paintings spanning the 13th to 16th centuries. Highlights include the jasper sarcophagus of Jaume II, an Arab tombstone and a painting of St George and the Dragon, which presents a background impression of what Palma may have looked like during the 15th century.

9 Museo Sa Bassa Blanca, Alcúdia

🔲 F2 🏠 C/del Coll Baix 🕐 10am– 6pm Wed–Sat, 10am–3pm Sun 🌐 msbb.org 💠

Set amid a beautiful rose garden and sculpture park, this museum houses contemporary art and a special collection of children's portraits from the 16th to 19th centuries.

10 Museu de Pollença

🔲 E1 🏠 C/Pere J. Cànaves Salas 🕐 10am–2pm Tue–Sat, 10am–1:30pm Sun 🌐 ajpollenca.net/ca/museu
Exhibits include prehistoric sculptures shaped like bulls and an impressive collection of works by local artists.

**Exhibits on display at
Museu de Mallorca, Palma**

as cult figures, surgical instruments, jewellery and gladiatorial gear.

7 Museu de Mallorca, Palma

The Palau Ayamans that houses this excellent museum *(p95)* dates from 1634. It was erected on the foundations of a 12th-century Arab house, which is still visible in the underground rooms of the museum. The superb collections present a full and well-documented range of Mallorcan artifacts, from the prehistoric up to fine examples of Modernista furniture. The Talayot figures – small bronze warriors – and re-creations of Neolithic dwellings are among the other highlights.

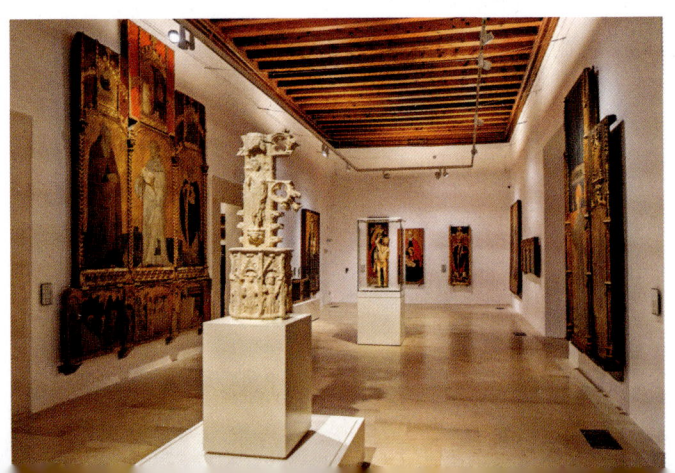

VILLAGES

1 Algaida
🗺 D4

Most people will pass through the outskirts of this small town on their way to Puig de Randa, but it is well worth making a stop here for some good restaurants, where the people of Palma come to dine at weekends. The Gordiola Glassworks (p131) are also nearby.

2 Alaró
🗺 D3

At one end of a scenic mountain road, under the shadow of the Castell d'Alaró, this pleasant little town dates from at least the time of the Moors. If you want to climb up to the castle, drive up to Es Verger restaurant and proceed on foot from there: the ascent takes about 45 minutes and the view en route is marvellous.

3 Santanyí

Founded in 1300 by King Jaume II, Santanyí (p124) was given a protective wall due to its proximity to the coast. Only part of that wall remains today, but it gives the place a certain character. For this reason, the town has attracted a large number of foreign dwellers, who have turned

it into a lively, rather cosmopolitan place. The fascinating art galleries around the main square are also well worth checking out.

4 Fornalutx

Often voted Mallorca's loveliest village (p102) – if not all of Spain's – this enchanting mountain enclave was founded by the Moors in the 12th century. The tiny village square is a friendly gathering place, but it is the heady views that visitors remember the most – up to the island's highest mountain and down into a verdant valley below.

5 Estellencs

Though today it is a pretty terraced town (p106) in a magnificent mountain setting, its old houses of grey-brown stone – left unplastered and unadorned – were essentially built for defence. Even the 15th-century church belfry was used as a place of refuge, as were most towers on the island.

6 Santa Maria del Camí
🗺 D3

A way station for weary travellers over the centuries, the village has a charming Baroque belfry, the Convent dels Mínims, a famed Sunday market and a quaintly traditional textile factory.

Fresh produce on sale at a market in Santanyí

7 Deià

Spilling down a steep hillside, Deià's *(p104)* earth-tone-coloured houses are, to many, the finest on the island. English poet and writer Robert Graves (1895–1985) lived here until his death, and he and his many artistic friends brought international fame to this picturesque village. Today, the tiny artists' retreat has been bought up by the wealthy, though it still retains its traditional appearance.

8 Binissalem

This small town *(p129)* is probably second only to Palma in the number and splendour of its stately mansions. Most of them date from the 18th century, when the surrounding area became the centre of a booming wine business. All of that stopped at the end of the 19th century, when phylloxera wiped out the vines. The local wine industry was revived in the late 20th century by the growing demand for good-quality local wines.

9 Capdepera

The well-preserved and extremely large medieval fortress that dominates the ridge above the town *(p121)* is the main reason to come to Capdepera. With its crenellated walls draped over the rolling hilltop, it is certainly a noble sight and one of Mallorca's finest

Flowers blooming in the lovely mountain town of Deià

castles. A fort has existed here in some form since at least the Roman times, and was used extensively during the 16th century to protect the local population from the regular raids by pirates.

10 Orient

Again, it is the mountain setting that dazzles here: this tiny, remote hamlet *(p106)*, with some 40 houses, a couple of restaurants and a church, has some of the finest views the island has to offer. It is also used as an excellent base for hikers or anyone who just wants to breathe the exhilarating air.

PORTS AND RESORTS

1 Port de Pollença

This family-friendly resort (p114), situated 6 km (4 miles) to the northeast of Pollença, beside a pleasant bay, is an attractive place with a long, sandy beach. Many retired foreigners have made the town their home.

2 Port de Valldemossa

C3

This tiny fishing port is one of the island's most secluded. The beach here is pebbly, and the houses are made of stone, as are the villas that are dotted all across the hill. Getting here involves a challenging drive down a series of hairpin bends

Boat on a slipway at Port de Valldemossa

along a cliff face and through pine forests. The lone restaurant, Es Port, is a treat, though only open for lunch.

3 Platja de Canyamel

H3

If a tranquil resort sounds enticing, this might be the place to come. Even in high season, it remains a quiet, family-oriented place – just a curving sandy beach backed by pine woods and a few tasteful hotels.

4 Cala Fornells

B4

A pleasant resort, Cala Fornells is made up of coves with turquoise water, sandy beaches and large, flat rocks on which to bask. Families flock here, and it's very good for snorkelling. The nearby town of Peguera has good nightlife.

5 Port d'Andratx

One of the classiest resort ports (p106) on the island, it is frequented by the Spanish king and other eminent visitors. Most of the restaurants and shops are on the south side of the port, while there is a prestigious sailing club on the north. The water is an inviting mix of azure and lapis, with touches of emerald, but the only beach is tiny.

**Enjoying the lovely sea view
from Port de Pollença**

6 Porto Cristo

Set around an old fishing harbour on the east coast, this family-friendly resort (p124) with an attractive centre and a harbourside beach has something for everyone. Choose from Blue Flag beaches, shops and restaurants, or the nearby archaeological sites and the famous Coves del Drac. There are also boat cruises from Porto Cristo that explore the eastern coastline. A number of watersport and safari options are available.

7 Cala Ratjada

This scenic port town (p124) is ideal for watersports of all kinds. Until recently the town was a quaint fishing village, and though it still has a working fishing port it is now rather overdeveloped. Fine beaches nearby include Cala Guyá, Cala Mezquida and Cala Torta, which allows nudists. There's also a ferry service to the neighbouring Balearic Island of Menorca from this port.

8 Port d'Alcúdia

Big and a bit brash, this resort town (p114) is a hit with the party-goers. But it is also one of the island's most popular holiday spots for families, featuring vast swathes of golden sand and calm, shallow waters. In addition to its great local beaches, the town offers excellent dining options and also has a large playground by the harbour.

9 Portopetro
📍 F6

Although on the verge of being swallowed whole by Cala d'Or (p124), this little fishing village has so far managed to retain its original flavour – possibly because there is no beach. Visitors can walk around and admire the slopes dotted by villas and the

boats in the small marina. There is only one hotel in town, which makes a good base from which to explore the island.

10 Port de Sóller

Backed by a pedestrian walkway, the lovely bay here (p103) offers calm waters for swimming, and a mix of hotels and nightlife venues catering to both young and old. Don't miss a ride on the antique tram that scoots to and from Sóller town.

**Vintage tram at
Port de Sóller**

AREAS OF NATURAL BEAUTY

with *patria* deleted some time ago by a liberal-thinking member of the new Spain. From here, there are dizzying views down to the sea below.

4 Gorg Blau
Created by seasonal torrents over millions of years, the ravine *(p112)* near Sóller and Puig Major is up to 400 m (1,312 ft) deep but only 30 m (98 ft) wide, with some sections never seeing daylight. An artificial reservoir here supplies water to Palma. Do not hike between the cliffs in winter.

5 Barranc de Biniaraix
C2
This is one of the island's most popular and breathtaking walks. Follow the cobbled pathways from the tiny village of Biniaraix up through the impressive scenery overlooked by Puig Major, Mallorca's highest mountain.

6 Parc Natural de Mondragó
One of the newer nature reserves *(p122)* established on the island, this one is part nature, part heritage site. It incorporates a full range of island terrains, from wooded hills to sandy dunes, as well as an assortment of rural

1 Península de Formentor
This jagged spur of the great Serra de Tramuntana range has been preserved and saved from overdevelopment mostly due to the fact that a large luxury hotel was built here *(p41)* in the 1920s. The drive out to the lighthouse from Port de Pollença is absolutely unforgettable.

2 Torrent de Pareis
A box canyon at the spot where the "Torrent of the Twins" meets the sea is one of the great sights of the island *(p116)*. The scale of the scene, with its delicate formations and colours, is amazing, and the sense of solitude is totally undisturbed, even by the crowds you will usually encounter here. The tunnel-like path from Cala Calobra was carved out in 1950.

3 Mirador de Ricardo Roca
B3
A chapel-like structure at this lookout point has the words *todo por la patria* (all for the fatherland) inscribed over its door – a remnant from Fascist times –

Overlooking the Platja de Mondragó

Hiking the rocky Barranc de Biniaraix

structures. Come here for hiking, bird-watching, picnicking, swimming or simply getting a feel for old Mallorca.

7 Cap de Cala Figuera Peninsula

◪ B5

Marked by a lonely lighthouse, this area is officially a military zone, but as long as it is not closed or guarded it is possible to walk out for a view of the bay. Nearby Portals Vells is a tranquil area, while Platja El Mago is a nudist beach.

8 Illa Dragonera

This uninhabited island *(p106)* is the place that encouraged the current conservation movement on the island. It is a great place to hike, take a picnic or just visit to admire the natural beauty. In the high season, ferries head here from either Sant Elm or Port d'Andratx.

9 Cap de Capdepera

◪ H3

The island's easternmost point is a great place to hike around, though the terrain generally permits little more than easy strolling. Visitors can go out to the lighthouse on its cape of sheer rock, or check out the pristine coves that lie lined up to the north and south, including Cala Agulla, Son Moll, Sa Pedruscada and Sa Font de sa Cala.

10 Parc Natural de S'Albufera

Roman naturalist Pliny wrote of Mallorcan night herons, probably from S'Albufera *(p114)*, being sent to Rome as a gastronomic delicacy. Most of the wetlands were drained for agriculture in the 19th century and what land was left has now been restored and turned into the largest wetlands nature reserve in the Balearics.

BEACHES AND COVES

four easily accessible sectors with section one being the most popular due to its proximity to many hotels and restaurants. The beach is ideal for kids as its shallow waters extend for a fair distance before the water gets deep.

4 Illetes
📍 C4

The western side of Palma Bay is generally upmarket, and "The Islets" typify the area's allure. Tiny islands, intimate coves, rocky cliffs and rolling hillsides are accentuated with attractive villas and a scattering of exclusive hotels on the waterfront.

5 Cala Tuent

On the wild northwest coast, where the opalescent hues of the massive cliffs and sea meet, Cala Tuent (p117) is probably the area's quietest beach, since it is bypassed by most of the crowds of tourists who come to see the nearby Torrent de Pareis (p116).

6 Cala Sant Vicenç

The area consists of three coves – Cala Sant Vicenç (p114), Cala

1 Es Trenc
📍 E6

This splendid beach is everyone's favourite, and weekends will find it very crowded with sun-worshippers who have made the trip from Palma. The rest of the week, it is the domain of nudists, nature-lovers, and neo-hippies. It remains the island's last undeveloped beach, interrupted only by the complex of vacation homes at Ses Covetes (p124).

2 Palmanova
📍 B4

Lying in the southwest of the island, Palmanova is only a few miles from Palma, with all its attractions. It makes an excellent staging post for family activities, such as visits to nearby Western Water Park or Aqualand Water Park (p79). The town's trio of superb sandy beaches are renowned.

3 Platja de Muro
📍 F2

This vast stretch of white sand on the north coast is one of the largest sand beaches in Mallorca, stretching almost 6 km (4 miles). The beach is split into

Relaxing on the beach at Cala Sant Vicenç

Barques and Cala Molins – with an appealing sense of intimacy. The first two have tiny but perfect beaches, gorgeous water and views. The third is down a hill, with a broader beach and more privacy.

7 Cala Llombards
F6

Near the town of Santanyí in the southeast corner of Mallorca is this pocket-sized beach surrounded by steep cliffs, towering pine trees and verdant shrubbery. This is one of Mallorca's most idyllic beaches: the bright white and soft sands are perfect for relaxing and the clear waters are generally calm. It is a great spot for both swimming and snorkelling, especially for younger kids. During the peak summer months, the beach is usually busy but rarely gets overcrowded.

8 Cala Figuera, Cap de Formentor
F1

Cutting a chunk out of the very end of the dramatic Península de Formentor, this cove lies at the bottom of a precipitous ravine. It is accessible either on foot – parking is up above,

Rocky cove at the bay of Cala Deià

just off the road that winds out to the lighthouse – or by boat, anchored offshore. Once there, the views of the surrounding cliffs are awesome, and the beach and water make it one of the island's most inviting swimming spots.

9 Cala Deià
C2

Hidden away among the mountains of the northwest coast, Cala Deià occupies a narrow rocky cove with a shingle beach. You can enjoy fresh (if pricey) grilled seafood at one of its two popular waterside restaurants.

10 Platja de Formentor
F1

Day-trippers from Port de Pollença come here, either by car or ferry, to enjoy the same pristine sands and pure waters as the guests of the grand Four Seasons Resort (p41). The unspoiled views here are among the very best on the island.

PARKS AND GARDENS

1 Botanicactus

📍 E6 🏠 Ctra. de Ses Salines a Santanyí, Ses Salines 🕐 10:30am–4:30pm Mon–Sat 🌐 botanicactus salines.com ↗

One of Europe's largest botanical gardens, Botanicactus has 12,000 cacti to admire, including a 300-year-old giant from Arizona. This popular spot has a wide variety of vegetation and biodiversity, including palms, bamboo groves and a large artificial lake that provides water to the tropical plants. Local flora is showcased through olive trees, pomegranates, almonds, pines, oranges, carobs and cypresses.

2 S'Hort del Rei

📍 L5

Gentle jets of water and bowl-shaped fountains characterize this lovely Moorish-influenced garden. As the name suggests, it was once the king's private garden, located near the walls of the Palau de l'Almudaina. Today, it is home to some eccentric modern sculpture.

3 Banys Àrabs Gardens

To the Moors, who came from an arid land where the oasis was the symbol of life, water was the very essence of a garden. The serene cloistered gardens surrounding the Banys Àrabs (p95) evoke that ideal – it was here that the wealthy owner would relax after his bath, and breathe in the fragrant air.

4 Jardins Sa Torre Cega

📍 H3 🏠 C/Juan March 2, Capdepera 🕐 10:30–noon Mon–Fri 🌐 fundacionbmarch.es/en ↗↗

Juan March was a Mallorcan-born magnate who allegedly made his fortune from illegal tobacco- and arms-trafficking. His grand mansion, built in 1916, near Cala Ratjada, has lavish grounds incorporating water gardens, pine woods and fruit groves. The gardens, located on the site of an ancient watchtower called the "Torre Cega", are also home to an impressive collection of over 40 works of modern sculpture, including a bronze by Rodin and a piece by Henry Moore.

5 Jardins d'Alfàbia

The island's best example of a profoundly Moorish garden (p50) dates back 1,000 years. Naturally, in all those centuries the various owners have added their own touches, resulting in Renaissance and Baroque elements in the design.

6 Parc de la Mar

With its artificial lake, section of city walls and great views, this park (p98) is a lovely place to stroll at any time. At night, the sparkling city lights of Palma and warm glow of the nearby cathedral and palaces make it especially magical.

Fountain at the lovely S'Hort del Rei

Pretty garden with the gazebo in the background, Son Marroig

7 Son Marroig

The famous Archduke Luis Salvador had many homes in Mallorca, but stunning Son Marroig (*p104*) was his favourite. The gardens, terraced in the ancient Moorish fashion, are deliberately left a bit wild, in keeping with the slightly rough look of the natural flora. All this vibrant nature neatly contrasts with the refinement of the architecture, especially the perfectly located gazebo that offers exquisite views of the coast.

8 Raixa

These gardens (*p104*) belonged to a cardinal, who liberally indulged his taste for collecting Classical statuary. However, only a fraction of his collection remains in the gardens; the rest now adorns the Castell de Bellver (*p26*) in Palma.

9 Parque de sa Feixina

🔲 J3

These gardens start where Avinguda de Argentina meets the Avinguda Gabriel Roca, and run up to Plaça La Feixina. The terraced lawns, fragrant trees and flowers, and attractive fountains and columns provide a welcome respite from the stone and asphalt of the newer parts of Palma.

10 Jardí Botànic de Sóller

🔲 C2 🚗 Ctra. Palma–Sóller, km 30.5, Sóller 🕐 Mar–Oct: 10am–6pm Mon–Sat; Nov–Feb: 10am–3pm Tue–Sat 🌐 jardibotanicde soller.org ⬈

Founded in 1985 for the conservation and study of Mediterranean flora, the garden is home to many endangered plants. Find medicinal herbs and flowers, wild flora and vegetables here.

WILDLIFE AND PLANTS

1 Mammals
Plenty of wild mountain goats can be seen in the remote areas of Mallorca. Rabbits, hares, hedgehogs, civet cats, ferrets, weasels and other small creatures may take longer to spot. The Mallorcan donkey is also increasingly rare – it has been cross-bred with its Algerian cousin, and there are only a handful of members of the pure species in existence.

2 Herbs and Shrubs
These include the wild grass (*Ampelodesma mauritanica)*, used for thatching and rope; the Balearics' only native palm, the dwarf fan palm; giant yucca and aloe; palmetto, used for basketry; and the giant fennel plant.

3 Wild Flowers
The island is home to more than 1,300 varieties of flowering plants, of which 40 are uniquely Mallorcan. Look out especially for the asphodel (with its tall spikes and clusters of pink flowers), the rock rose in the Serra de Tramuntana and the Balearic peonies. Spring and early summer are

Attractive asphodel wild flower

usually the best times to see them in all their colourful bounty.

4 Trees
The mountain areas are defined by pines, junipers, carobs and evergreen holm oaks, while palms, yews and cypress have been planted on the island since time immemorial.

5 Insects
In the warmer seasons, there are plenty of colourful butterflies in the wooded areas of the island, as well as bees, mayflies and hornets. In hot weather, especially among cedars, hikers will be treated to the noisy song of the cicadas.

6 Songbirds
Species breeding here, or stopping for a visit in the spring or summer, include stonechats, larks, warblers, the stripy hoopoe, swifts, partridges, buntings, finches, pipits, shrikes, turtle doves, swallows, the brilliantly coloured European bee-eater and the inimitable nightingale.

7 Reptiles and Amphibians
Frogs, salamanders, tortoises, snakes and lizards abound in Mallorca. But perhaps the most notable two species on the island are the endangered ferreret, a toad found in the

Mallorcan donkey in a meadow

Serra de Tramuntana, and Lilford's wall lizard, which thrives on the islets offshore.

8 Cultivated Plants
Some of the flowering plants you see around the island are cultivated for decorative purposes, such as oleander, purple morning glory, bougainvillea, *Bignonia jasminoides* (trumpet vine – used as cover for pergolas), geranium and wisteria. Grapes, citrus fruit and olives have been part of Mallorca's landscape since Roman times.

9 Birds of Prey
The island's numerous dashing Eleonora's falcons form an important part of the world's population – you can see them around the Formentor lighthouse (p41). The peregrine falcon, too, breeds in these parts, and you can spot black vultures, red kites, eagles, buzzards, harriers and owls.

10 Marine Birds
Bird-watchers come from all over Europe to see rare migrants, especially at the S'Albufera wetlands (p114). Notable species include marsh harriers, herons, egrets, stilts, bitterns and flamingos. Seagulls, sandpipers, cormorants, ospreys and terns live along the rocky coasts.

Greater flamingos in the S'Albufera wetlands

TOP 10 PLACES TO SEE WILDLIFE

1. Península de Formentor
This jagged spur of mountain and rock (p40) is circled by various seabirds, including the stunning Eleonora's falcon.

2. Illa de Cabrera
This sun-bleached archipelago (p30) off the island's south coast is famous for its colony of Lilford's wall lizards.

3. Gorg Blau
This remote gorge (p112), surrounded by mighty peaks, is the best place to spot the rare black vulture.

4. S'Albufera
A rare patch of wetland, S'Albufera (p114) is a haven for many types of bird, including Montagu's harriers, moustached warblers, crakes and herons.

5. Sineu
In fields near Sineu (p130) you could spy the brightly coloured hoopoe, one of Mallorca's handsomest birds.

6. Illa Dragonera
An uninhabited island off the west coast, Illa Dragonera (p106) has been a nature reserve since 1988 and is famous for its spectacular sea birds, notably birds of prey, including the largest colony of Eleonora's falcons in the world.

7. Lluc
The mountains near Lluc (p38) are the last refuge for the rare and endangered ferreret toad.

8. Es Pla
It's rare to catch sight of the nightingale but you may hear this shy bird singing in any part of Es Pla (p128).

9. Colonia de Sant Jordi
The saltpans behind this resort (p123) have a distinctive birdlife, including flamingos and black-winged stilts, and abundant marine life.

10. Parc Natural de Mondragó
This lovely nature reserve and park (p122) attracts a wide variety of migratory and resident birds.

DRIVES AND HIKES

1 Sa Calobra
☑ D2
Driving anywhere around Puig Major *(p116)* affords great views and challenges your driving skills. With looping turns that twist down the mountainside, this road has earned its name, which translates as "The Snake". This 30-minute drive leads to a tiny settlement, where you can explore the dazzling beauties of the box canyon created over thousands of years by surging torrents.

2 Andratx Round Trip
☑ B3–4
Take this two-hour-long drive from the main highway north of Andratx to the Mirador de Ricardo Roca, Banyalbufar, then Mirador de Ses Ànimes *(p106)* for panoramic views. Turn towards La Granja, then pass down through Puig-punyent, Puig de Galatzo, Galilea, Es Capdellà and back to Andratx.

3 Old Road to Sóller
☑ C3
This 45-minute drive over the Coll de Sóller mountain pass, with its 57 hairpin bends, is Mallorca's most exhilarating. But it is worth it to experience what life used to be like before the tunnel opened.

4 Bunyola–Orient–Alaró
☑ C3–D3
Another extremely narrow road that threads its way along precipitous mountain ridges. It's an hour-long drive with stops along the way. The town of Orient is a pretty eagle's nest of a place, and the glimpse of Castell d'Alaró *(p105)* is impressive.

5 GR-221 Long-Distance Route
☑ B4–E1
Around 135 km (84 miles) long, this beautiful walk follows the length of the Serra de Tramuntana on the island's northwest coast, taking about six to eight days to complete.

6 Sant Elm to La Trapa
☑ A4
This popular three-hour walk leads to an old Trappist monastery. A shorter route is signposted beside the cemetery on the Sant Elm–Andratx road.

7 La Reserva
☑ B3 🚶
This reserve on the slopes of Puig de Galatzó has Mallorca's most diverse collection of plants. A 3.5-km- (2-mile-) long walking trail takes in waterfalls and springs.

**Hiking a trail on the
GR-221 route**

8 Puig de Santa Eugènia
📍 D3

It take about two hours to reach the top of Puig de Santa Eugènia. From the village of Santa Eugènia, walk to Ses Coves. From here, a series of tracks takes you up to a pass and the cross on the summit of Puig de Santa Eugènia, affording fine views.

9 Archduke's Mulepath
📍 C3 🏠 Near Valldemossa

Red markers take you up to a viewpoint and a high plateau before dropping down through a wooded valley. This six-hour-long walk is for experienced hikers only.

10 Pollença to Puig de Maria
📍 E1–2

The signpost to Puig de Maria is at km 52 on the main road from Palma to Pollença. It's a 90-minute hike from here to the top of the Puig de Maria. A sanctuary, set on an isolated hill, offers views of the Península de Formentor.

**Walking on a trail leading
to Puig de Maria**

TOP 10
PEAKS

Towering Puig de Massanella

1. Puig Major
📍 D2 🏠 Serra de Tramuntana
The island's highest mountain is 1,447 m (4,747 ft) high *(p116)*.

2. Puig Sant Salvador
📍 F5 🏠 Serra de Llevant
The Llevant's second-highest peak (510 m/ 1,673 ft) is home to the well-loved Santuari de Sant Salvador *(p123)*.

3. Puig de ses Bassetes
📍 D2 🏠 Southwest of Massanella
This peak (1,216 m/3,990 ft) is near the Gorg Blau reservoir.

4. Puig d'es Teix
📍 C2 🏠 Valldemossa
A mountain (1,062 m/3,484 ft) in the heart of verdant Tramuntana.

5. Puig Galatzó
📍 B3 🏠 Puigpunyent
This mountain (1,025 m/3,363 ft) overlooks the valley of Puigpunyent.

6. Puig Roig
📍 D1 🏠 North of Lluc
Puig Roig (1,002 m/3,287 ft) is named for its reddish colour.

7. Puig Caragoler
📍 D1 🏠 Camí Vell de Lluc
Access this mountain (906 m/2,972 ft) via the Camí Vell de Lluc trail.

8. Puig Morell
📍 G3 🏠 Serres de Llevant
This is the highest peak (560 m/ 1,837 ft) in the Serres de Llevant.

9. Puig de Randa
📍 E4 🏠 Central Plain
The only high point (543 m/1,781 ft) on the Central Plain.

10. Puig de Massanella
📍 D2 🏠 Serra de Tramuntana
The highest mountain (1,367 m/4,485 ft) that can be climbed on the island.

SPORTS AND OUTDOOR ACTIVITIES

1 Hiking
Mallorca's most challenging long-distance footpath is the GR-221, which weaves a dramatic route across the mountains of the Serra de Tramuntana. It takes up to eight days to complete the full trail. There are many other shorter trails leading through stunning scenery.

2 Football
There are two professional football teams in Mallorca – Real Mallorca and Atlético Baleares – both of which play in Palma during the season, which runs from early September to April.

3 Canyoning
A key target for canyoning enthusiasts is the Torrent de Pareis, a dramatic gorge that cuts through the mountains backing onto Sa Calobra. The area can be dangerous and is suitable only for experienced canyoners with the proper equipment.

4 Cycling
Groups of avid cyclists, decked out in colourful lycra, are seen all over the island, from the mountain roads to the narrowest stone-walled lanes of Es Pla. It is easy to rent bicycles in most towns.

5 Rock Climbing
There are many compelling challenges for climbers on the rocky cliffs that abound along the length of the Serra de Tramuntana, from Sóller in the west to the end of the Península de Formentor in the east. Parks and tourist offices offer published guidelines for tackling the wilderness.

6 Fishing
There are a number of boats that will take people out fishing, particularly from the port towns that still fish commercially, such as Portocolom (*p124*). The bays of Pollença and Alcúdia (*p44*) are also popular for fishing.

7 Horse-Riding
Mallorcan farmers are proud of their well-bred horses, and horse-riding is a very popular pastime. The best place to get in the saddle is in the Serres de Llevant, home to several riding schools.

Cyclists heading to Cap de Formentor

8 Paragliding

Seeing the island from the air is a thrilling and unforgettable experience, and there is no better way to do it than from on high in a paraglider. Mallorca now has several tour operators and paragliding schools, with options for all levels.

9 Golf

There are more than 20 world-class golf courses scattered all around the island. Courses are prevalent near all the the big resorts, though some of the finer hotels have their own and many more have putting greens. Golf Son Termens (golfsontermes.com), Capdepera Golf (golfcapdepera.com) and Club de Golf Vall d'Or (valldorgolf.com) offer great golf course options.

10 Bird-Watching

Nature reserves are best for bird sightings, especially those on the northeastern coast, such as S'Albufera (p114) and the Península de Formentor (p40). Spring and autumn are optimal times to visit, when migratory birds use Mallorca as a staging post between Europe and Africa. The isolated islands of Illa Dragonera (p106) and Cabrera (p30) are also excellent for spotting.

TOP 10 MARINE ACTIVITIES AND WATERSPORTS

Riding a pedalo

1. Jet Skiing
You can rent a jet ski from resorts at Magaluf and Port d'Alcúdia (p114).

2. Scuba Diving
The waters off Mallorca tend to have mixed visibility – but the waters off Illa Dragonera (p106) are crystal clear.

3. Windsurfing
The windy waters in the bay beside Port de Pollença (p114) are very popular with windsurfers.

4. Boating
The finest cruises are the two- or three-hour cruises along the dramatic southeast coast (p121).

5. Diving
The clear coastal waters off Estellencs (p106) provide some of the best diving conditions on the island.

6. Sea-Kayaking
Several companies offer sea-kayaking trips with a favourite spot being the bay edging Port de Sóller (p103).

7. Water Skiing
All of Mallorca's larger resorts cater for would-be water skiers.

8. Paddle Boarding
Popular with locals and visitors, paddle boarding is offered at bigger beaches. SUP boards are available for hire.

9. Pedalos
You can rent large and brightly coloured pedalos in the shape of cars and yachts at most large resorts.

10. Sailing
The myriad coves and bays of Mallorca are perfect for sailors – and sailing.

FAMILY ATTRACTIONS

1 Tram from Sóller to Port de Sóller

📍 C2 🕐 Tram departs every hour until noon then every half hour daily (from Sóller: 8am–8:30pm; from Port de Sóller: 8:30am–9pm) ↗

Board a slow tram at the little station above the main square of Sóller, which takes visitors 5 km (3 miles) through the town and along the water's edge to Port de Sóller.

2 Karting Magaluf

📍 B4 🏠 Ctra. de la Porrasa, Magaluf, Calviá 🕐 Feb–Easter: 10am–6pm Wed–Sun; Easter–Oct: noon–8pm daily 🌐 kartingmagaluf.com ↗

An exhilarating karting experience for the family. Safe and secure tracks and

Go-karting at Karting Magaluf

go-karts are suited to children as young as three years old, and everyone is made to feel like a champion. A large terrace bar is available for snacks, drinks and ice creams.

3 The Rafa Nadal Museum Xperience

📍 F4 🏠 Ctra. Cales de Mallorca, s/n, Manacor 🕐 10am–6:30pm daily 🌐 rafanadalmuseum.com ↗

Sports enthusiasts will enjoy this immersive museum. Interactive and high-tech exhibits bring to life sports from Formula 1 to tennis – look out for Rafael Nadal's huge collection of trophies and racquets. The centre also has a sports complex, tennis school, hotel and places to eat.

4 Rancho Grande

📍 F3 🏠 Son Serra de Marina, Ctra. Arta–Alcúdia, km 13.7 🌐 rancho grandemallorca.com ↗

The largest horse ranch on Mallorca offers rides for people of all ages and evening entertainment for the whole family. There are also wagon rides, a children's play area, a mini-zoo, and a bar and restaurant.

**Disembarking from the
tram at Port de Sóller**

5 Palma Aquarium

⬛ C4 🏠 C/Manuela de los
Herreros i Sorà, 21 ⏰ 9:30am–
6:30pm daily (last entry: 5pm)
🅦 palmaaquarium.com ↗

This aquarium is home to a range
of flora and fauna from the world's
largest oceans and the Mediterranean
Sea. Ecosystems of about 700 species
and 8,000 specimens are re-created
at this wonderful aquarium.

6 Katmandu Park

⬛ B4 🏠 Avda. Pedro Vaquer
Ramis, 9, Magaluf, Calviá ⏰ Hours
vary, check website 🅦 katmandu
park.com ↗

This popular theme park, featuring
an enormous and very fun upside-
down house, has been named the
second most popular family attraction
in Mallorca. The park is full of interactive games that will have the whole
family competing against each other,
as well as a 4D cinema, a waterpark and
a mini-golf course.

7 Golf Fantasía

⬛ B4 🏠 C/Tenis, 3, Palmanova,
Calviá ⏰ 10am–6pm daily (Apr, May
& Oct: to 10pm; Jun–Sep: to midnight)
🅦 golffantasia.com ↗

Just metres from the beach, Golf
Fantasía offers family fun with three
18-hole courses set among exciting
locations – think caves, wooden
bridges, waterfalls and tropical
gardens. There is also a terrace
snack bar to fuel your round.

8 Aqualand

⬛ D4 🏠 Autovía Palma–
Arenal, km 15, El Arenal ⏰ May–Oct:
10am–5pm daily (Jul & Aug: to 6pm)
🅦 aqualand.es

Mallorca's largest waterpark is a real
hit with the kids – both tourists and
local. There are swimming pools, water
flumes and chutes galore, with one
resembling a giant, wriggling snake.

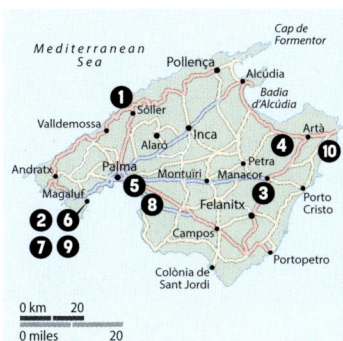

9 Western Water Park

⬛ B4 🏠 Ctra. Cala Figuera–Sa
Porrasa, 2–22, Magaluf ⏰ Late May–
Sep: 10am–5pm daily (Jul & Aug: to
6pm) 🅦 westernpark.com ↗

Mallorca's most popular waterpark
has a kitsch western theme with a
saloon and a candy parlour. It is also
home to the highest waterslide on
the island – the so-called "Beast".

10 Caves

Young adventurers will love
exploring the hundreds of caves found
around Mallorca, especially the Coves
d'Artà *(p121)*, which exit onto the open
sea. At the Coves del Drac *(p46)*, the
pitch-darkness is exciting, but the very
young may find it a little scary, or get
frustrated by the silence.

**Admiring the stalactites
at Coves d'Artà**

NIGHTS OUT

1 Theatre and Opera
Mallorca has a thriving and often overlooked theatrical scene. Regular performances are held in both grand halls, like the Auditòrium de Palma, and intimate venues, such as the Theatre Sans (*estudizeroteatre.com*). The heart of Mallorca's theatre scene is the Teatre Principal (*teatreprincipal.com*), which has hosted theatre, musicals, opera, *zarzuela* and more for over 350 years.

2 Cocktail Bars
Mallorca takes cocktails seriously and you can enjoy perfect creations at venues like U Gallet (*linktr.ee/ugallet*) in Pollença or Capricho Bar (*Carrer Benito Jerónimo Feijóo*) in Puerto Portals. For the best bars, head to Palma. Sip imaginative concotions at the Brassclub (*brassclub.com*) or drink in the Speakeasy-style Door 13 (*Carrer de les Caputxines*). Ever tried a cactus-based tipple? Agabar (*C/de la Fàbrica*) takes the crown for tequila- and mezcal-laced cocktails.

3 Outdoor Cinema
Make the most of Mallorca's balmy summer nights and catch a flick in the moonlight. Watch Spanish, Catalan and English-language films under Palma's cathedral at Cinema a la Fresca (*Parc de ses Estacions*) or, for a more retro feel, try the drive-in movie nights that are part of the Evolution Mallorca International Film Festival (*evolutionfilmfestival.com*).

4 Night Markets
For the opportunity to pick up some local produce and souvenirs without the blazing sun, join the locals at an evening market, or "Fira Nocturna". These regularly occur in Palma, Palmanova, Puerto Alcúdia and Santanyí, among others, and fall somewhere between a market and a fête, with live music, traditional dancing and kids' entertainment.

5 Live Music
Mallorca is becoming a live music hotspot. Hear the best classical sonatas at the Auditorium de Palma (*auditoriumpalma.com*) or see future stars at local venues like The Shamrock (*p118*). Make a note of the Mallorca Live Festival (*mallorcalivefestival.com*), which pulls in big headliners and local acts every June.

6 Sunset Party Boats
As night falls, the peaceful boats bobbing in Mallorca's harbours transform into the hottest party zones. Take a trip from either Platja de Palma or Port d'Alcúdia where live DJs and free-flowing libations make for a fun evening.

7 Late-Night Openings
Mallorca has many excellent venues and museums, and some stay open late into the evening. The Es Baluard (*p60*) complex is open till midnight daily, while Palma's cathedral (*p22*) hosts evening tours during the summer months.

A stall selling wicker items at a local night market

Art-lovers should look out for the *Nit de l'Art* (Night of Art) in September, where galleries, museums and cultural spaces stay open late for this city-wide event.

8 Spectacular Shows
Flamenco has a passionate following in Mallorca and the best local performers strut their stuff at Tablao Flamenco Alma (*tablaoflamencoalma*). For something completely different, catch the perennially popular Pirates Adventure show (*piratesadventure.com*). where acrobatics, theatre and dance combine in one breathtaking show.

9 Tapas Trails
You can't visit Spain without tasting some tapas, and fortunately you can find it everywhere in Mallorca. A great starting point is the La Ruta Martiana i Palma; held every Tuesday, many of the restaurants and bars around Palma Old Town offer cut-price tapas and drinks.

10 Nightclubs
It's not hard to find a party in Mallorca: the island has some of the best clubs in the world. Magaluf is party central and clubs such as BCM Mallorca (*bcmmallorca.com*) and Bananas (*Carrer dels Pinzons*) lead the way with all-night parties and superstar DJs. Or, dance the night away in Palma. Try Lio Mallorca (*liogroup.com*), a restaurant, cabaret venue and fun nightclub rolled into one.

A busy street around a nightclub in Magaluf

TOP 10 CHIRINGUITOS BARS

Patrons at Puro Beach

1. Puro Beach
Dress to impress at this chic bar *(p100)*.

2. S'Arenal
🅟 C2 🅐 Ctra. Faro, s/n
🅦 grupomarport.com
Pair Mediterranean dishes with some of the fruitiest cocktails and smoothies.

3. Ca's Patró March
🅟 F2 🅐 C/Sa Cala, 16
A renowned bar in Cala Deia with great views and even better food.

4. Ponderosa Beach
🅟 F2 🅐 Casetes des Capellans, 123
🅦 ponderosabeach.com
This is a vibrant bar on Platja de Muro.

5. Chiringuito de Cala Sa Nau
🅟 F5 🅐 C/de Cala Sa Nau
🅦 calasanau.com
It's all about the freshest seafood here.

6. Mai Mai Surf Bar
🅟 C4 🅐 C/dels Pins, 17A
🅦 maimaisurfbar.com
Sip on sangria made by the owners.

7. S'Ona beach
🅟 F6 🅐 Parking playa, Santanyí
Try some of the best paella here.

8. El Chiringuito Sa Foradada
🅟 C2 🅐 Diseminado Sa Foradada, 2
This popular spot has great views overlooking Sa Foradada.

9. Il Chiringo
🅟 B4 🅐 Paseo Mar/p. Nova, 19
🅦 ilchiringo.com
A DJ and resident mixologist ensure the good vibes flow at this bar.

10. 5Illes Beach & Sunset
🅟 E6 🅐 Platja de S'Estany
🅦 5illesmallorca.com
Sip a sundowner on the Estanys beach.

LOCAL DISHES

A plate of *tumbet*, a ratatouille-style dish

1 Tumbet
The vegetables that go to make up this *ratatouille*-style stew can vary widely, depending on the season, but it will classically comprise a selection from among the following: aubergine (eggplant), bell peppers, courgettes (zucchini), onions, cabbage and potatoes. The seasoning is mainly garlic.

2 Vi de la Casa
Mallorca is now enjoying a decided upswing in its wine production, and you can generally depend on the house wines being very good. The reds are considered the island's best at the moment, being robust and aromatic, though some whites attain a lively fruitiness.

3 Arròs
Arròs (rice) dishes include the familiar *paella Valenciana*, saffron rice with a mixture of vegetables, chicken and sausage; *arròs brut*, a meaty rice stew; and *arròs negre*, rice with seafood cooked using squid ink.

4 Frit Mallorquí and Llom amb Col
Frit is a hugely popular local dish dating back to the 14th century. It is made with meat offal or fish, cooked in oil with potatoes, onions and some vegetables. It is at its savoury best in some of the more traditional market towns of Es Pla. *Llom amb col*, pork wrapped in cabbage, is equally traditional and substantial.

5 Sobrassada
Mallorca's most prized paprika sausage, *sobrassada*, comes from the island's famous small black pigs. It is tender, flavourful and tinged red from spices, and there are various versions of it, including a *sobrassada* pâté for spreading on toast.

6 Sopes Mallorquinas
By far the best of Mallorca's *sopes* (soups) is fish soup, a hearty stew of shellfish and white fish in a broth flavoured with garlic and saffron. It may also contain rice or pasta for added body and seasonal vegetables. Other soups common on the island are concoctions of vegetables and mixed meats, often seasoned with garlic.

**Delicious Mallorcan
pastry, *Ensaïmada***

7 Ensaïmades
These unbelievably light and flaky spiral shaped pastries have been the pride of the island since being introduced in the 17th century. Enjoyed any time of day, they can be dusted with icing sugar or filled with a variety of ingredients such as custard, chocolate, candied fruits or jam.

8 Sea Bass Baked in Rock Salt
The Mallorcan version of this classic is the pièce de résistance wherever it is served. The salt pack keeps the moisture and flavour inside, but the delicate, succulent fish is left with a hint of saltiness to add piquancy.

9 Pa amb Oli
This is the most popular Mallorcan (and greater Catalonian) snack – a regional version of the more internationally known bruschetta. The basic item is brown bread rubbed with garlic, then smeared with fresh tomato, drizzled with olive oil and sprinkled with salt. To this basic recipe, anything can be added – usually ham and/or cheese.

10 Canya and Hierbas
Canya is the term for local draught beer, and *hierbas* is a famed herbal liqueur, made with fresh local herbs collected from the hills. *Cervesa* (beer) tends to be of the Pilsner type, though in Palma you can find a local variety that is black, fizzy and bitter.

***Sopes Mallorquinas
with a glass of wine***

TOP 10
TAPAS TYPES

1. Pickled
The easiest finger-nibbles: olives (sometimes very salty), miniature pickles and possibly pearl onions.

2. Marinated
All manner of seafood, including anchovies, sardines and shellfish, steeped in pale green olive oil.

3. Padrones
These are small green peppers, fried with salt, garlic and olive oil.

4. With Mayonnaise
Patatas bravas, fried potato cubes with mayonnaise and spicy red sauce, are a favourite. As is aïoli, a pungent mix of garlic and mayonnaise.

5. On Bread
The signature bread snack *pa amb oli* is brown bread with olive oil, tomato and other toppings.

6. Egg-Based
Truita espanyol is a potato, egg and onion omelette, served by the slice. *Revuelto de huevos*, scrambled eggs, is popularly served with prawns.

7. Fried
Chipirones and calamari rings are also favourites, along with croquettes.

8. Grilled or Roasted
From snails roasted with garlic to grilled baby squid, octopus, aubergine, kebabs and sweet bell peppers.

9. Stewed or Steamed
As well as *tumbet*, steamed shellfish, broad green beans and artichokes shouldn't be missed.

10. Cured
A cured favourite is salted cod. Sliced cured ham is also available widely, along with local sausage, *sobrassada*.

Cured sausage, *sobrassada*

WINERIES

1 Son Prim, Sencelles
D3 · Camí de Inca
W sonprim.com
This family-run bodega produces some superb award-winning wines. They specialize in red wines, with Syrah, Cabernet Sauvignon and Merlot vines, and the local grape Manto Negro.

2 Bodegues Ribas, Consell
D3 · C/de Muntanya, 2
10am–6pm Mon–Sat; book tours in advance · W bodegaribas.com
Established in 1711, the oldest bodega in Mallorca has been with the Ribas family throughout. It is now an organic estate, where they grow many of the island's indigenous grape varieties.

3 Bodegas Can Majoral
D4 · Carrero del Campet, 6
W canmajoral.com
One of the pre-eminent producers of organic wines in Mallorca, this bodega is passionate about indigenous grapes such as Prensal, Collet and Gorgollasa. They also host the annual grape harvest at full moon.

4 Bodega Biniagual, Binissalem
This historic wine-producing village has been beautifully restored after a period of neglect, and this small, self-sufficient estate (p132) enjoys an idyllic setting.

Once again producing wines in time-honoured tradition, its Veran and Grand Veran wines are particularly good. Book tours in advance.

5 Celler Tianna Negre, Binissalem
D3 · Camí des Mitjans · W tianna negre.com
The striking architecture here reflects the bodega's reputation for being at the vanguard of innovation. Tasting tours can be arranged if booked in advance.

6 Bodega Ramanyà, Santa Maria del Camí
D3 · Camí de Coscois · W bodega ramanya.com
Try the unusual cavas from this delightful boutique winery, run by the affable Toni Ramanyà. A visit (advance booking required) includes entry to his superb ethnographical museum, where 2,000 artifacts, including traditional carriages and carts, are housed.

7 Bodegas Mesquida Mora, Porreres
E4 · Camí de Sant Joan
W mesquidamora.com
The winery is owned by the fourth generation of the Mesquida family.

Wines at Bodegas Macià Batle, Santa Maria del Camí

Vineyard set on a
picturesque hillside

They create biodynamic wines from
indigenous and imported grape varieties. Advance booking is required.

8 Bodegues Castell Miquel, Alaró

D3 ⌂ Ctra. Alaró–Lloseta, km 8.7
⊙ Hours vary, check website
ⓦ castellmiquel.com ☐

Phytoneering entrepreneur Professor
Popp has produced some complex
wines here. The restored estate's terraces are linked by steep stairways
that are illustrated on the wine labels.

9 Galmes i Ribot, Santa Margalida

F3 ⌂ Ctra. Santa Margalida–Petra,
km 2.4 ⓦ galmesiribot.com

The Ribot-Galmés family transformed
their estate in 1997, planting vines with
the aim of creating top-quality wines.
Their bold approach, mixing old vines
with new techniques, has paid off.

10 Bodegas Macià Batle, Santa Maria del Camí

D3 ⌂ Camí de Coanegra, s/n
⊙ 9am–6:30pm Mon–Sat
ⓦ maciabatle.com ☐☐

One of the biggest bodegas on the
island, this is a stop on the Wine
Express tourist train. They produce a
range of good wines, which are available for tastings or to buy in the shop.

TOP 10 WINE SHOPS AND DELIS

1. La Vinoteca, Palma
C4 ⌂ C/Pare Bartomeu Pou, 29
ⓦ lavinoteca.info/es/vinos
A superb selection of wines from
producers across the island.

2. DiVino, Port d'Andratx
A4 ⌂ C/Alejandro Cardunets, 1
☎ 971 674669
Tuck into treats from the deli and
sip on Mallorcan and Spanish wines.

3. Pan y Vino, Palma
C4 ⌂ C/Ausiàs March, 22
☎ 613 809285
A bodega-style shop selling
Mallorcan wines and tapas.

4. Colmado la Montaña, Palma
N4 ⌂ C/Jaume II, 27 ☎ 971
712595
Shop for *sobrassada*, as well as
local charcuterie and cheeses here.

5. Mallorcària, Palma
N4 ⌂ C/de Santa Eulàlia, 11
ⓦ store.mallorcaria.com
Great choice of local wines, craft
beers and Mallorcan items.

6. Sa Cisterna, Alcúdia
F2 ⌂ C/Cisterna, 1 ☎ 971
548606
A shop with olive oil, wines, local
meats and cheeses, plus a bar area.

7. El Paladar, Palma
L2 ⌂ C/de Bonaire, 21
ⓦ elpaladar.es
Specialists in wine, cheese and ham
from around the Balearic Islands.

8. Mallorca Delicatessen Mateu Pons, Palma
N3 ⌂ Plaça del Marquès
del Palmer, 7 ⓦ mallorcadeli
catessen.com
A shop for gourmet Mallorcan goodies.

9. S'Hort de Cartoixa, Valldemossa
C3 ⌂ C/de ses Filoses, 26
Deli serving the best Mallorcan produce.

10. La Pajarita, Palma
M4 ⌂ C/Sant Nicolau, 2
ⓦ lapajaritabomboneria.com
A charming 19th-century store
with a confectionery and a deli.

PLACES TO SHOP

Traditional whistels
at Sineu Market

1 Sineu Market
In a historic town in the central plain (p130), this market, held on Wednesdays, is one of the island's biggest agricultural fairs, where local produce is traded. Pottery, leather and lace are among the goods sold.

2 Manacor Pearls
The unprepossessing town of Manacor is notable for its manufactured goods, with pride of place going to its world-famous artificial pearls (p132). The standards of fabrication are exacting, as a free tour of the factory will reveal, along with the variety of shapes and shimmering colours indistinguishable from true pearls.

3 Sa Pobla Market
🅿 E2
The town's central square is the place to be on a Sunday morning, to experience an authentic country market. Visitors will find the freshest organic produce on the island – strawberries and potatoes are specialities here – and get to sample the local spicy tapas. Clothing, accessories and plants are also on offer here.

4 Wineries
Top-quality wine production in Mallorca is on the rise, with more and more of the island's vineyards (p84) dedicated to fine wines rather than the table wines for which the island was historically better known. Most bodegas offer tastings and sell their bottles on the premises.

5 Inca
Though Inca is a working town, it is the island's centre (p128) for the production of leather goods. Many outlets offer leather jackets, handbags, shoes and a host of other stylish items. The outdoor Thursday market is also well worth a visit.

6 Avinguda Jaume III, Palma
🅿 K–L3
This elegant, arcaded avenue is one of Palma's main streets for chic boutiques, shoe stores and good local shops such as Persepolis for antiques.

7 Sant Nicolau and Plaça Major
🅿 N3
The pedestrian shopping streets in central Palma form a warren behind

Shopping for trinkets
on Plaça Major

Bar Bosch on the main Passeig des Born, with a good selection of shops. In this area, around Plaça Major, there are many speciality gift shops.

8 El Corte Inglés, Palma
🗺 K3–L3 🌐 elcorteingles.es
Palma has two branches of Spain's own department store, El Corte Inglés Alexandre Rosselló and El Corte Inglés Jaume III, where the quality and prices are firmly upmarket.

9 Gordiola Glassworks
Housed in a Neo-Gothic building, this place *(p131)* is worth a prolonged visit. Visitors can learn the art of glass-blowing by watching the professional glass-blowers engaged in their art, then spend an hour in the museum upstairs and at least another hour browsing through the vast warehouse shops offering their prodigious output of beautiful glassware.

10 Artesanía Textíl Bujosa, Santa Maria del Camí
The festive *robes de llengües* (tongues of flame cloth) are made here *(p132)*, in every possible colour and design. Watch them being made |at this out-of-the-way spot and buy bolts of fabric or ready-made items.

TOP 10
MARKETS

Colourful pottery items, Sineu

1. Palma Daily Markets
Passeig de la Rambla for flowers, Plaça Mayor, Mercat del Olivar, Mercat de Santa Catalina, Mercat de Pere Garau and Mercat de Llevant for produce, and Llotja del Peix for fish.

2. Palma Weekly Markets
This lively flea market takes place in Palma's Son Fuster neighbourhood every Saturday until 2pm.

3. Villages on Sunday
A great day for many village markets: Consell, Valldemossa, Santa Maria del Camí, Inca, Sa Pobla, Pollença, Muro, Alcúdia, Porto Cristo, Portocolom, Felanitx and Llucmajor.

4. Villages on Monday
Monday markets are held at Manacor, Montuïri, Caimari, Calvia and Lloret.

5. Villages on Tuesday
Some of the lesser-known villages have markets on Tuesday: Campanet, Alcúdia, Artà, Santa Margalida and Porreres.

6. Villages on Wednesday
A big day for markets, especially at Sineu. Others at Andratx, Selva, Port de Pollença, Capdepera, Petra, Colònia de Sant Jordi and Santanyí.

7. Villages on Thursday
Markets at Inca, as well as Ariany, S'Arenal, Consell, Campos, Ses Salines.

8. Villages on Friday Morning
Inca for leather, Binissalem, for wine, and Son Severa, Llucmajor and Algaida.

9. Villages on Friday Afternoon
Alaró and Can Picafort.

10. Villages on Saturday
This is a big market day for the island.

MALLORCA FOR FREE

1 Castell de Bellver, Palma
This curious, circular castle (*p26*), which is one of Palma's most popular attractions, allows visitors to enter for free every Sunday.

2 Ancient Sites
Many of Mallorca's ancient sites do not charge visitors an entrance fee, including the Poblat Talaiòtic (Talayotic village) in S'illot, and the necropolis on the Son Real estate.

3 Traditional Festivals
The island's festivals (*p90*) offer all kinds of free events. Watch demons dodge dragons in the *correfoc* ("fire-running"), catch some live music, enjoy fireworks or battle with Christians.

4 Far de Porto Pí, Palma
📍 C4 🏠 Ctra. Arsenal, 3E
🌐 farsdebalears.org ⬦
Built in 1617, the Far de Porto Pí is the third-oldest operational lighthouse in the world and holds a commanding position on Palma's waterfront. The sight was declared a National Historic Monument in 1983 and has an adjoining museum. Free hour-long guided tours of the exhibit at the lighthouse are given from Wednesday to Saturday between 10am and 3pm (book in advance online).

5 Sa Llotja, Palma
Originally used as a maritime trading exchange, this 15th-century Gothic masterpiece (*p98*) now functions as a free exhibition space. However, the architecture here is the main draw, with numerous pillars dramatically spiralling up to a rib-vaulted ceiling.

6 Nit de l'Art (Art Night), Palma
🌐 nitdelartartpalma.com
The Nit de l'Art (Art Night) takes place every year on the third Thursday of September, when the galleries and

Participants celebrating the *correfoc* in Alaró

**Circular Castell
de Bellver, Palma**

museums of Palma's old quarter host exhibitions, performances, installations and urban interventions. It has become one of the most popular and exciting free art events on the island.

7 Museo Fundación Juan March, Palma

Set in an elegant 17th-century mansion, this museum (p98) holds an impressive collection of artworks by some of the most prestigious Spanish artists such as Picasso, Miró and Dalí, and does not charge an entry fee. A number of free workshops and talks are also offered.

8 Centro Cultural Can Balaguer, Palma

🗺 M3 🏠 C/de la Unió 📞 971 225900

There's no charge to enter this restored 17th-century mansion, which is home to a cultural centre. It hosts free temporary exhibitions covering local art, history and culture.

9 Local Museums

Entry is free at many local museums in Mallorca, including many of the museums in Pollença (p114), Muro (p130) and Manacor (p130).

10 Museu Sa Bassa Blanca, Alcúdia

This art museum (p61) has a truly magnificent rural setting, and offers free entry to its famous collection of historic children's portraits (known as the "Nins"). Visitors can also view the museum's stunning coffered ceiling from 4 to 5:30pm on Thursdays by appointment.

**White camel
sculpture at
Museu Sa Bassa
Blanca, Alcúdia**

TOP 10 BUDGET TIPS

1. Holiday Packages
Fantastic deals can be had on package holidays, especially if dates are flexible. The low season has the best deals.

2. EMT Travel Pass
🅦 emtpalma.cat
Ten-ticket bus passes offer better value for the visitors who are travelling around Palma.

3. Local Tourist Offices
The local tourist offices in Palma and across the island provide free maps, and lists of free events and activities.

4. Discounts at Museums
Most museums offer discounts for children, seniors, students and the unemployed, as long as you can produce valid documentation.

5. Parking
The larger towns of Mallorca have metered street parking with a per-hour rate. Parking is often free in the afternoon.

6. VAT Refund
Non-EU residents can get the IVA (VAT or sales tax) returned at participating stores for purchases of more than €90.

7. Walking Tours
There are many free walking tours that explore Palma, its monuments, and even some museums.

8. Picnics
Sunny weather, superb markets and tasty, good-value local produce make this a great destination for picnicking.

9. Menú del Día
Set-price lunch menus are usually excellent value, and can also put some of the fanciest restaurants within the reach of limited budgets.

10. Local Wines
Mallorca's impressive range of local wines are not only cheaper than comparable wines from elsewhere, but can be a better complement to the food.

FESTIVALS

1 Revetlla de Sant Antoni Abat

17 Jan

One of Mallorca's most unusual festivals, in honour of the patron saint of animals. For two days in Palma, Sa Pobla and Muro, pets are led through the town to be blessed at the church. Elsewhere, dancers drive out costumed devils, and crowds circle bonfires and eat pastries of spinach and marsh eels.

2 Festes de Sant Sebastià

Last fortnight in Jan

Palma's patron saint is honoured with fireworks, dragons, processions, street concerts and beach parties in Palma and Pollença in one of the island's most colourful and exuberant festivals.

3 Maundy Thursday

Mar or Apr

Setmana Santa (Holy Week) in the capital city is observed by a solemn procession of some 5,000 people parading Christian icons in Palma.

4 Festa de l'Àngel

Sun after Easter

Villages across Mallorca celebrate the Feast Day of the Angel with a pilgrimage to their local shrine.

The biggest event takes place in Palma's Castell de Bellver (p26) but the pilgrimage from Alaró (p62) to its castle is also very colourful.

5 Festa de Nostra Senyora de la Victòria

From 2nd Sun in May

Port de Sóller is the venue for a mock battle between Christians and Moors, in commemoration of a skirmish in which Arabic corsairs were routed in 1561. Expect lots of rowdy, boozy fun, brandishing of swords and firing of antique guns.

6 Nit de Sant Joan

23 Jun

This famously raucous festival is one of the biggest on the island – with the grandest festivities in Palma. Hordes of masked devils, spectacular firework displays and pulsating drums make this an exhilarating night of revelry.

7 Día de Mare de Déu del Carme

15 & 16 Jul

This celebration of the patron saint of seafarers and fishers takes place in various coastal settlements, including Palma, Port de Sóller, Colònia de Sant Pere, Portocolom and Cala Ratjada.

**Fireworks during the Festa de
Sant Bartomeu**

Boats are blessed, torches are lit (as
at Port de Sóller), and sailors carry
effigies of the Virgin Mary.

8 Festa de Sant Jaume
Week leading up to 25 Jul
Alcúdia honours its patron saint
St James with the usual summer
revelry, including folk dancing,
fireworks and parades featuring
an icon of the saint and various
religious symbols.

9 Mare de Déu dels Àngels
2 Aug
This long mock battle between the
Christians and the Moors takes place
in Pollença. The town spends a whole
year preparing for the event, at which
hundreds of youths dress up.

10 Festa de Sant Bartomeu
Until 24 Aug
The highly charged Nit de Foc (Night
of Fire) marks the end of a fortnight-
long fiesta for Sant Bartomeu, Sóller's
patron saint. People dressed as devils
with forks and firecrackers playfully
chase locals around Plaça Constitució,
while pyrotechnicians organize a
spectacular smoky atmosphere
and fireworks display.

**Maundy Thursday
procession in Palma**

TOP 10
FIGURES IN MALLORCA'S
RELIGIOUS HISTORY

1. Lluc
Legend recounts that over 800 years
ago a young boy named Lluc discovered the effigy of the Madonna and
presented it to the nearest monk *(p38)*.

2. Gaudí
The devout architect was responsible
for the restoration of Palma Cathedral
and other holy sites on the island.

3. Knights Templar
A rich and powerful brotherhood
of Christian military monks had
their headquarters in Palma *(p98)*.

4. Inquisition Judges
The Inquisition was introduced
to the island in 1484 and led to at
least 85 people being burned alive.

5. Xuetes
The name given to the Jews who
were coerced by the Inquisition into
converting to Catholicism.

6. Junípero Serra
An important 18th-century monk,
missionary and colonialist, born in
the town of Petra *(p129)*.

7. Santa Catalina
The island's only homegrown saint,
Santa Catalina Thomás was born in
1531 in Valldemossa *(p33)*.

8. Cardinal Despuig
The 18th-century cardinal developed
the more opulent side of church life
when he built his home, Raixa *(p104)*.

9. Bishop Campins
The driving force behind
the renewal of the
monastery at Lluc as
a pilgrimage site.

10. Ramon Llull
The 13th-century
Mallorcan writer and
philosopher founded
several religious
ceremonies and
festivals on the island.

**Statue of
Ramon Llull**

AREA BY AREA

A street in Pollença

PALMA

Since being founded by the Romans, Palma, the capital of Mallorca, has evolved over the centuries from a coastal village into a cosmopolitan city. It was shaped by Byzantine and Moorish occupiers who created its medieval core and the beautiful baths still seen today. In 1983, Palma became the capital of the newly created Autonomous Community of the Balearic Islands and today it is a thriving metropolis with around 500,000 inhabitants. Indeed, its attractive streets, historic buildings and mix of restaurants, bars and shops ensures that Palma remains a city that captivates all visitors as it once captivated Jaume I, who, after conquering it in 1229, is supposed to have described it as the "loveliest town that I have ever seen".

Central Palma

For places to stay in this area, see p144

Flemish tapestries at the Palau de l'Almudaina

1 Palau de l'Almudaina

🗺️ M5 🏛️ C/Palau Reial 🕐 Hours vary, chech website 🌐 patrimonio nacional.es 🔲🔲

Having been a royal palace for over 1,000 years, this building's style reflects its long, fractious history with an uneasy blending of Moorish and Gothic elements. Visitors can take a tour of the palace premises.

2 Banys Àrabs

🗺️ N5 🏛️ C/Can Serra, 7 📞 637 046534 🕐 10am–6pm daily 🔲

This 10th-century brick *hammam* (bathhouse) is one of the few architectural reminders left of a Moorish presence on Mallorca. A small chamber has survived in its original form, with a dome supported by columns and what was once underfloor heating. This would have been the *tepidarium*, the lukewarm room; there would have also been a hot room and a cold plunge pool.

3 Museu de Mallorca

🗺️ N5 🏛️ C/de la Portella, 5 📞 971 177838 🕐 Hours vary, call ahead 🔲

It is worth the entrance fee just to see inside the building, a 17th-century palace built on the foundations of one of Mallorca's earliest Moorish houses. The museum contains some fascinating exhibits, providing a quick overview of Mallorca from prehistory to the 20th century. There's also a fine collection of paintings by local artists, ranging from religious medieval works to island landscapes. Some gorgeous examples of Modernista furniture are also on display – in particular, an interesting console with a daringly asymmetrical design.

Greater Palma

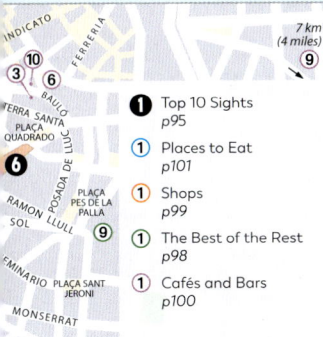

4 Casal Solleric

L3 Passeig Des Born, 27
10am–8pm Tue–Sat, 11am–2:30pm Sun & public hols casalsolleric. palma.cat

A splendid Italianate edifice, the Casal Solleric was built for a family of olive-oil merchants in 1763. Now a cultural centre, it also has a gallery, café and bookshop. The house stands at the top of the Passeig des Born avenue, which was created in the 19th century on a dried-up riverbed. Similar to Barcelona's famous tree-lined street LasRamblas, this is Palma's main promenade and the venue of large-scale cultural events.

5 Plaça Weyler

N3

Several interesting examples of Palma's Modernista output are found in this buzzing square. The Gran Hotel, a landmark site here, was Palma's first luxury hotel when it opened in 1903. Designed by eminent Catalan architect Lluís Domènech i Montaner, it was the building that began the desire for Modernista in the city and is now an excellent art gallery, CaixaForum, with a permanent display of paintings by Hermen Anglada-Camarasa, and a major venue for temporary exhibitions. Across the street is the wonderful façade of the Fornet de la Soca pastry shop *(p59)* next to the old-fashioned Bar Central.

6 Basílica de Sant Francesc

P4 Plaça Sant Francesc
971 712695 10am–6pm Mon–Sat

During the Middle Ages, this Gothic-style church was one of the most fashionable churches in Palma, and to be buried here was a major status symbol. Aristocratic families competed with each other by building ever more ostentatious sarcophagi in which to place their dead. The church was remodelled in the 17th century after being damaged by lightning. The dark interior contains many fine works of art. Next to a 17th-century statue of the Madonna is the carved figure of the medieval writer and philosopher Ramon Llull, who is buried in the church. In front of the basilica is a statue of Junipero Serra, a Franciscan monk, Catholic colonialist and native of Mallorca, who went to California in 1768 and founded Los Angeles and San Francisco.

PALMA'S URBAN BEACH

Stroll east along Palma's seafront promenade and you will arrive at the city's beach, Platja de Can Pere Antoni. This long stretch of yellow sand is popular with local families and has a swanky beach club at each end. Just beyond the beach is the scenic Portixol, an upmarket seafront suburb with great restaurants.

High central nave at La Seu: Palma Cathedral

7 La Seu: Palma Cathedral

Dominating the port, this is the second-largest Gothic cathedral *(p22)* in the world and the island's most-visited building.

8 Museu d'Art Sacre de Mallorca

🗺 M5 🏠 C/Mirador, 5 🕐 Apr–Oct: 10am–5:30pm Mon–Fri, 10am–3pm Sat; Nov–Mar: 10am–4pm Mon–Fri, 10am–3pm Sat 🌐 museuartsacrede mallorca.org ↗

The 17th-century Palau Episcopal houses a diocesan museum. On display are some items from Mallorcan churches, and a selection of stunning majolica tiles. Noteworthy are a 1468–70 painting of St George slaying the dragon in front of Palma's city gate by Pere Nisart; Bishop Galiana's panel that shows the life of St Paul (depicted holding a sword); the Gothic pulpit in a Mudéjar style; and the sarcophagus of Jaume II, which stood in the cathedral until 1904. The palace itself, which is built around a large courtyard, adjoins the city walls.

9 Castell de Bellver

One of Europe's remarkable castles *(p26)* was actually a prison for 700 years and now houses an excellent museum.

10 Fundació Miró Mallorca

This museum *(p28)* showcases the prolific career of Catalan artist Joan Miró in all its depth and variety. It's a highlight of any trip to Palma.

Fornet de la Soca on Plaça Weyler

A WALK AROUND OLD PALMA

Mid-Morning

Start in Plaça Joan Carles I, at the top of the **Passeig des Born**. From here, walk east on La Unió to **Plaça Weyler** to buy pastries at the Fornet de la Soca *(p59)* and see exhibitions in the Gran Hotel.

Climb the steps to the right of the Teatre Principal to reach the **Plaça Major** *(p86)*. This arcaded square is filled with artists and performers. Stop for a drink in one of the cafés.

Come out of the Plaça along Carrer Sant Miquel. Stop at the charming **Església de Sant Miquel** and the **Museu Fundació Juan March** *(p98)*.

Now double back through Plaça Major to view the façades of **L'Aquila** and **Can Rei** *(p98)*. Go down Carrer Argenteria to visit the **Església de Santa Eulàlia** *(p98)*, and then Carrer d'En Morei to take in **Ca N'Oleza** *(p98)*.

Afternoon

Continue on to Carrer Miramar, past the glorious **Palacio Ca Sa Galesa** hotel, to exit at the broad seawall, where you can look up at **La Seu cathedral** *(p22)*.

Visit the cathedral and **Palau de l'Almudaina** *(p24)*, then go down to the **S'Hort del Rei** gardens *(p70)*. Finally, stroll up the Born and have a snack at **Bar Bosch** on Plaça Rei Joan Carles I, or head to one of the restaurants *(p101)* in the square for lunch.

The Best of the Rest

1. Església de Santa Eulàlia
N4
Built in the mid-1200s in Gothic style, this church was remodelled in the 19th century.

2. Parc de la Mar
M6
This park, next to the cathedral, is a popular spot, with a lake, cafés and open-air concerts.

3. Ca N'Oleza
N5 C/d'En Morei, 9
This aristocratic mansion has fabulous wrought-iron railings, a Gothic stairway and graceful balustrades.

4. Sa Llotja
K4 Passeig de Sagrera 971 711705 11am–2pm & 5–9pm Tue–Sat
This handsome, 15th-century seafront building houses a cultural centre.

5. Fundación Bartolomé March
M4 C/Palau Reial, 18 Hours vary, chech website fundacion bmarch.es
The sculpture collection here features works by Hepworth, Rodin and Moore.

6. L'Aquila/Can Rei
N3
These are two striking examples of Palma's Modernista architecture.

L'Aquila combines elements of Catalan Modernista with Viennese tendencies, while Can Rei owes much to the influence of Antonio Gaudí.

7. Can Vivot
N4 C/Can Savellà, 2
Can Vivot is one of Palma's grand courtyards with its fine Corinthian columns and balustraded balcony. Its sumptuous library, filled with scientific instruments dating from the Enlightenment era, is sometimes open.

8. Museu Fundación Juan March
N3 C/Sant Miquel, 11 10am–6:30pm Mon–Fri, 10:30am–2pm Sat march.es/es/palma
The collection here includes works by Picasso, Dalí, Miró and Juan Gris.

9. Templar Gate
P5 C/Temple
A fortified gate marks the former entrance to the 13th-century headquarters of the Knights Templar, built when the wealthy brotherhood was in full power. The buildings are now privately owned.

10. Plaça de Cort
N4
With its ancient olive tree and elegant façades, including the town hall, this is one of Palma's nicest squares.

Relaxing under the ancient olive tree, Plaça de Cort

Shops

Clothing and homeware at Rialto Living

1. Rialto Living
📍L4 ⌂C/Sant Feliu, 3 🕐11am–8pm Mon–Sat 🌐rialtoliving.com

This ultra-stylish lifestyle store stocks everything from books and fashion to beds and sofas. There's also an attractive café on the ground floor.

2. Santa Catalina Market
📍C4 ⌂Plaça Navegació, s/n 🕐7am–5pm Mon–Sat 🌐mercatdesanta catalina.com

The stalls at this municipal market are piled with fresh produce, and the café-bars are a great spot for breakfast or tapas.

3. Fine Books
📍N5 ⌂C/d'En Morei, 7 🕐10am–2pm & 3:30–7:30pm Mon–Fri, 10am–2pm Sat

This chic Old Town shop is full of all manner of second-hand and antique books, mostly in English.

4. Louis Vuitton
📍L4 ⌂Passeig Des Born, 19 🕐10am–9pm Mon–Sat 🌐louisvuitton.com

A wide range of upmarket clothes and accessories are sold in an elegant setting here.

5. Estilo Sant Feliu
📍L4 ⌂C/de Sant Feliu, 11B 🕐11am–3pm Mon–Sat 🌐estilosantfeliu.com

A shop selling traditional Mallorcan decorative ceramic and textile goods as well as olive-wood products, many of which are handmade.

6. Colmado Santo Domingo
📍M4 ⌂C/S. Domingo, 1 🕐10:15am–7:30pm Mon–Sat 🌐colmadosanto domingo.com

Every foodstuff made on the island is here. Note the impressive array of cured meats strung from the ceiling.

7. Alpargateria La Concepción
📍L2 ⌂C/Concepción, 17 🕐10am–2pm & 5–8pm Mon–Fri, 10am–2pm Sat 🌐zapateriamallorca.com

This shop sells handcrafted sandals and espadrilles made on the island.

8. Rouge Mallorca
📍L4 ⌂Plaça Frederic Chopin 🕐11am–7pm Mon–Sat 🌐rougemallorca.com

Shop for top-quality vintage designer bags and accessories here.

9. Isabel Guarch
📍M3 ⌂Plaça del Mercat, 16 🕐11am–7pm Mon–Fri 🌐isabelguarch.com

A bijou jewellery shop offering unique Mediterranean-inspired pieces designed by Mallorcan Isabel Guarch.

10. Bagatela
📍M4 ⌂Passeig des Born, 24 📞971 715312 🕐May–Sep: 11am–8pm Mon–Sat; Oct–Apr: 11:30am–6:30pm Mon–Sat

This is a one-stop shop for those looking for gifts and crafts.

Cafés and Bars

Exquisite flower and fruit decoration at Abaco

1. Abaco
L4 C/San Juan, 1 8pm–12:30am Sun–Thu, 8pm–1am Fri & Sat bar-abaco.es

A most romantic setting for drinks: an ancient courtyard and lush garden with perfumed air and soft candlelight.

2. Café Roma
M1 Baró de Pinopar 971 720321 7am–midnight daily

An unpretentious and inexpensive place popular with locals. It serves delicious Spanish and Mallorcan fare and a variety of beers.

3. Molta Barra
P4 C/del Pes de la Farina, 12 7pm–12:30am daily (to 2am Fri & Sat moltabarra.es

Set in Palma's trendy Sa Gerreria neighbourhood, this bar attracts locals for its excellent tapas and great music.

4. Cappuccino Sant Miquel
N1 C/Sant Miquel, 53 cappuccinograndcafe.es

Since it started operating in the 1990s, this small chain has been known for fast service and fresh food. It offers great coffee and light lunches.

5. Bar España
N3 C/de Can Escursac, 12 1–4pm & 6:30pm–midnight Mon–Sat barespanya.es

Close to Palma's Plaça Major, this traditional tapas bar is popular with locals and tourists alike. It offers an excellent beer menu.

6. Bar Flexas
P3 C/Llotgeta, 12 6:30pm–1am Tue–Thu, noon–2am Fri & Sat barflexas.com

This well-established vintage-style bar attracts a big crowd for its excellent food and LGBTQ+-friendly nights.

7. Café La Lonja
L4 C/de la Lonja, 2 10am–1am Mon–Fri, 11am–1am Sat & Sun cafelalonja.com

Enjoy lovely views of the historic Old Town from the patio of this great bar and café as you sip on a drink.

8. Ca'n Joan de S'aigo
P4 C/C'an Sanç, 10 8am–9pm daily canjoandesaigo.com

Since 1700, this Rococo-style café has been serving delicious chocolate, *orjata* (almond milk), ice cream and pastries. Note that it can get busy.

9. Puro Beach
C4 C/Pagell 1, Cala Estancia 11am–midnight daily purobeach.com

A spectacularly situated bar that benefits from a pleasant sea breeze. The DJ plays cool house music.

10. Gaudí
P4 Plaça de la Quartera, 5 Kitchen: 9am–11pm Mon–Sat; bar: 7pm–2am daily gaudipalma.com

This welcoming café and bar is especially popular on weekends, so make sure to arrive early. Try cocktails and traditional dishes.

Places to Eat

1. Can Eduardo
J5 ⌂ C/Contramuelle Mollet, 3
🕐 1–10pm Tue–Sat, 1–3:30pm Sun
caneduardo.com · €€€

Located above Palma's wholesale fish market, this is one of the best restaurants on the island for fresh seafood.

2. La Bóveda
L5 ⌂ C/Boteria, 3 🕐 Hours vary, check website Feb laboveda.makro.rest · €€

Housed in an old building, this charming restaurant serves Basque-Castilian food, including tapas.

3. Casa Gallega
M1 ⌂ Avda. del Comte de Sallent, 19 🕐 Hours vary, check website casagallegamallorca.com · €€

Queue up to enjoy classic Galician cooking here. Options include a *menú del día*, tapas and à la carte.

4. Marc Fosh
N2 ⌂ C/de la Missió, 7A
🕐 1–2:30pm & 7:30–9pm Tue–Sat
marcfosh.com · €€€

This relaxed restaurant is one of Palma's most popular spots.

5. Celler Sa Premsa
N1 ⌂ Plaça Bisbe Berenguer de Palou, 8 🕐 Noon–4pm & 7:30–11pm Mon–Sat (Jul & Aug: Mon–Fri) cellersapremsa.com · €€

Come here for classic dishes such as cabbage rolls with pork, and paella. It also has an excellent selection of wines.

6. Tast Unión
M3 ⌂ C/Sant Jaume, 6 🕐 1pm–midnight Mon–Sat tast.com · €€

Hidden down a narrow side street off Jaume III, this sophisticated, intimate gem serves up creative tapas and high-quality Mediterranean cuisine.

7. Ca n'Ela
L5 C/de la Mar, 16 871 776653
🕐 1–4pm & 7:30–10:30pm Mon–Sat · €

One of Palma's best vegan restaurants offering great-value set menus for lunch and dinner.

8. Adrián Quetglas
K2 ⌂ Passeig Mallorca, 20 971 781119 🕐 Hours vary, call ahead · €€€

The Michelin-starred eponymous chef creates adventurous contemporary cuisine. The set tasting menus are superb.

9. Duke Restaurant
S1 ⌂ C/Soler, 36 🕐 7–11pm Mon–Sat dukepalma.com · €€

Relaxed and informal, Duke serves healthy international dishes including an excellent three-course menu. It also has a patio for alfresco dining.

10. Cuit
K3 ⌂ Hotel Nakar, Avda. Jaume III, 21 🕐 1–4pm & 7–11pm Mon–Sat; brunch: noon–3pm Sun nakarhotel.com/cuit-restaurant · €€€

Cuit serves creative Mallorcan-inpsired dishes, all made with local produce.

Dining area with superb views at Cuit

SOUTHWEST COAST

The southwest is one of Mallorca's most naturally diverse regions, with soaring mountains, rugged cliffs and deep forests. In winter, the mountains shield the central plain from the fierce *Tramuntana* wind and absorb most of the island's rain and snow, while in summer, they provide a cool retreat from the heat of Palma. Dotted among this natural beauty are historical towns and charming villages, including Port d'Andratx, Deià and Sóller, and extravagent resorts filled with every kind of modern luxury.

1 Fornalutx
D2

This stone village is wonderfully situated, enjoying a splendid view of towering Puig Major (p116) – Mallorca's highest peak – and of the steep valley that sweeps down into orchards of orange and lemon groves. Silence reigns, except for the lazy sound of goat and sheep bells. The town seems to cling to its perpendicular foundations, with accommodation and dining options making the most of the panorama. You can get here by car, but a better choice is the pine-scented hike up from Sóller, passing through the even tinier Biniaraix (p106).

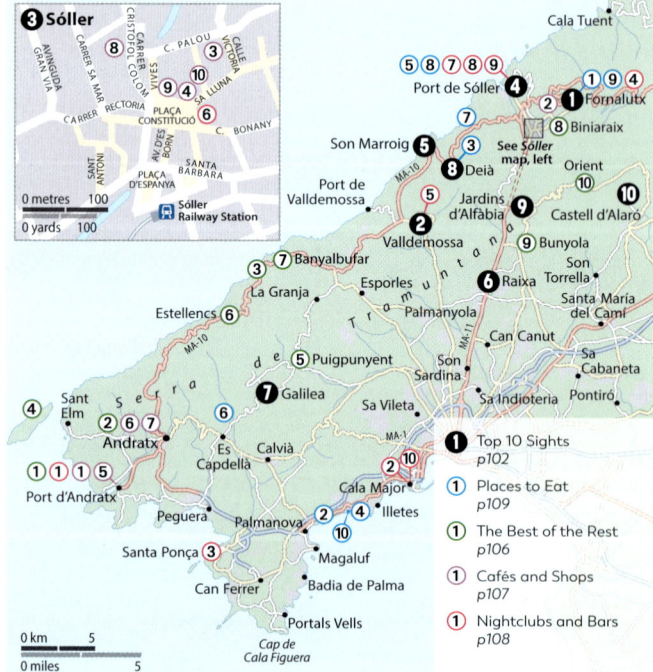

For places to stay in this area, see p145

2 Valldemossa

It was at the Carthusian monastery in Valldemossa *(p32)*, one of Mallorca's prettiest hilltop towns, that the famous Polish composer Frédéric Chopin and his lover, writer George Sand, spent one dramatic and unhappy winter in the early 19th century. Their experiences resulted in Sand's infamous book *A Winter in Majorca*, both a scathing indictment of the island's people and their ways, and a poetic rhapsody in praise of the natural beauties of the town and the island.

3 Sóller

The town's *(p36)* name reputedly derives from the Arabic *suliar* – "golden valley" – due to the gorge being famous for its orange groves. The most notable buildings include Modernista Banco de Sóller, now Santander Bank, and the Neo-Gothic church of Sant Bartomeu, both the works of a disciple of Antoni Gaudí. Sit in Plaça Constitució soaking up the atmosphere, or visit Can Prunera art gallery or the Natural History Museum. The town's vintage train provides a superb ride through the mountains to Palma.

Historic tram passing the busy town centre, Sóller

Palm trees and sunloungers on a beach, Port de Sóller

4 Port de Sóller

7 C2

This small resort is situated 5 km (3 miles) from Sóller. Set around a beautiful horseshoe-shaped bay, it has vibrant festivals and the only sandy beach of any size along the western coast. Its excellent natural harbour is the starting point for boat trips along the coast and a good base for walks – there is a short climb to the Cap de Gros lighthouse in Port de Sóller, which has great panoramic views over the island.

Gazebo as seen from the mansion, Son Marroig

5 Son Marroig

C2 ⌂ Ctra de Valldemossa–Deià 📞 971 639158 🕐 9:30am–2pm & 3:30–4:30pm Mon–Sat

High above the sea, with its famous Neo-Classical gazebo imported from Italy, this L-shaped mansion was fashioned by Archduke Luis Salvador (p70). Much admired in Mallorca, the archduke is remembered here with a museum. In the gardens, you can sit in the white Carrara marble rotunda and gaze at the Na Foradada ("pierced rock") Peninsula, jutting out to sea with an 18-m (59-ft) hole at its centre. The mansion has accessible facilities.

6 Raixa

C3 ⌂ Palma–Soller road, km 12 📞 971 237636 🕐 10am–3pm Tue–Sat

During the 18th century, Mallorcan country homes became a symbol of prestige, and this one, built by Cardinal Antonio Despuig, is one of the finest. The cardinal was an antiquarian and adorned his Italianate estate with Classical statuary to complement the grand Neo-Classical staircase. The parterres are laid out in the Italian taste of the day, with Classical touches such as fountains and medieval references.

Statue on a staircase, at Raixa

7 Galilea

B4

Perched high up in the mountains, this quiet village is a slice of pre-tourism Mallorca with its traditional stone houses and wild goats (with bells on). The village is surrounded by dense forests and tall mountains, and is the starting point for numerous hikes.

8 Deià

C2

Deià is mostly associated with the English author and poet Robert Graves, who moved here in 1929 and stayed for most of the next 56 years, making the place popular with other writers, such as Alan Sillitoe and Roger McGough, and artists such as Picasso. Graves' house

THE FRENCH CONNECTION

Before the Sóller Tunnel opened in 1997, the mountain-ringed Sóller Valley was almost cut off from the rest of the island. Thus, the north of the island carried out more commerce with France than with Palma. Sóller enjoyed a brisk orange trade with France, and their special relationship continues now.

(lacasaderobertgraves.org), C'an Alluny, has been turned into a museum of his artifacts and letters. Overlooking the village is the late 15th-century parish church of Sant Joan Baptista, where the writer's grave can be visited. The parish museum is next door, and down the hill is a small museum.

9 Jardins d'Alfàbia

This oasis of heavenly peace high in the mountains was designed by Arab landscape architects 1,000 years ago as an image of Paradise. The gardens *(p50)* have been reworked over the centuries, mostly with Gothic and Italian Renaissance touches, but the medley of fountains, terraces and groves are still essentially Moorish in style.

10 Castell d'Alaró

🅓 D3 📞 971 940503

The original castle was built over 1,000 years ago by the Moors and refurbished by Jaume I in the 13th century. It is mostly rubble now, but the lofty position seems unconquerable enough. At the bottom of the trail is Es Vergé, a rustic inn; from here you can follow well-beaten paths along the cliff.

Admiring the view en-route to Castell d Alaró

A TOUR OF DRAMATIC PROMONTORIES

Morning

Start at **Andratx** *(p106)* and take the coastal road, the MA-10, north. At the point where the road encounters the coastline is the **Mirador de Ricardo Roca** viewpoint and the **Es Grau** café. At **Estellencs** *(p106)*, there are some good places to shop and eat.

As the road leaves the town and climbs, there is a point to the left, which offers a good view. Next stop is the magnificent **Mirador de Ses Ânimes** *(p106)*.

At **Banyalbufar** *(p106)*, note the remarkable terraced hillsides. A little way on, there are signs for **La Granja**. Head there for lunch and a good look around the mansion and grounds.

Afternoon

After lunch, there is more historic sightseeing to be had at lovely **Valldemossa** *(p32)*, including the former monastery, modern art museum and the Old Town.

Carrying on north, pop into **Son Marroig** and then wind around into glorious **Deià**, great for a stroll.

Continuing on to Mallorca's smallest village, **Lluc-Alcari**. Finally, head for the main square in **Sóller** *(p36)* to have a drink, then take the quaint tram down to **Port de Sóller** *(p103)* for dinner in one of the great fish restaurants lining the harbour.

The Best of the Rest

1. Port d'Andratx
📍 A4

This spot is one of Mallorca's classiest seaside resorts.

2. Andratx
📍 B4

A sleepy town, Andratx comes alive on market day (Wednesday). Set on the outskirts of town, the Centro Cultural Andratx hosts international artists and organizes regular exhibitions.

3. Mirador de Ses Ànimes
📍 B3

The best mirador (viewpoint) on the entire coast is crowned by the Torre Verger (p57), which visitors can climb, just as watchmen did for centuries, keeping a fearful eye out for pirates and marauders.

4. Illa Dragonera
📍 A4

A narrow, rocky island lying at an angle to the coast near Sant Elm, Dragonera has been a nature reserve since 1988 and is home to a wide variety of wild flowers and birdlife, including cormorants, Cory's shearwater and the world's largest colony of Eleonora's falcon. According to legend, the island is visited nightly by dragons. However, its name has more to do with the shape than mythical beasts. A rocky path runs between its two headlands, both marked by lighthouses. Ferries from Sant Elm operate in summer, allowing visitors to explore the island for hours.

5. Puigpunyent
📍 B3

Lying in the shadow of Puig de Galatzó, this pretty mountain village is the base for visiting La Reserva nature park (p74).

6. Estellencs
📍 B3

This is a tiny, picturesque mountain town with restaurants and shops. There is also a seaside area around a beach, where the snorkelling is good.

7. Banyalbufar
📍 B3

Built by the Moors using dry-stone walls, the town's terraces speak of human ingenuity in creating farmlands out of inhospitable cliffs. There are a few nice hotels, some cafés, restaurants and artisan shops, and a beach.

8. Biniaraix
📍 C2

A smaller sibling to Fornalutx (p102), this charming village clings to the hillside near the Barranc de Biniaraix gorge, offering great views.

9. Bunyola
📍 C3

This is a pretty place in the foothills of the Serra de Tramuntana. Inside its church is a cherished 14th-century image of the Virgin in alabaster.

10. Orient
📍 D3

Those who make the hair-raising drive from Bunyola to this hamlet at the foot of Puig d'Alfàbia can have a choice of walks, including one to Castell d'Alaró (p105).

Hiking along a scenic path in Banyalbufar

Cafés and Shops

Outdoor seating at Cappuccino, Port d'Andratx

1. Cappuccino, Port d'Andratx
📍 A4 🏠 Avda. Mateu Bosch, 31
🌐 cappuccinograndcafe.es
With a waterfront location by the fishing port, and lovely sunset views, this café serves great snacks and coffee, as well as excellent breakfasts. There's also free Wi-Fi.

2. Cooperativa Agrícola Sant Bartomeu, Sóller
📍 C2 🏠 Ctra de Fornalutx, 8
📞 971 630294
This cooperative, founded in 1899, produces four delicious types of olive oils: soft Mallorquina, fruity Arbequina, spicy Picual and Coupage (a mix of the other three).

3. Café Scholl, Sóller
📍 W1 🏠 C/Victòria 11 Maig, 9
📞 610 625419
Tuck into tasty homemade cakes and sandwiches in this charming, retro-style café, which also has a small plant-filled terrace. At lunchtime, you can enjoy quiches, moussaka and more, with plenty of choice for vegetarians and vegans.

4. Mademoiselle, Sóller
📍 W1 🏠 C/de sa Lluna, 18
📞 697 434215
Colourful and creative fashions and accessories for women are elegantly displayed in this stylish shop.

5. Tricia's, Port d'Andratx
📍 A4 🏠 C/Saluet, Local 2
📞 971 671922
This glitzy boutique stocks fashion from top international labels, such as Missoni, I love Moschino, and M.i.h. jeans.

6. Ca'n Nadal, Andratx
📍 B4 🏠 C/Juan Carlos I, 7
📞 971 100850
Founded in 1872, this pastry shop offers delicious baked treats such as *mantecados* (shortbread), *cremadillo de cabello* (sugar-coated millefeuille), *pastel de chocolate* (iced chocolate cake with walnuts) or *tortaletta rechesol y frutos secos* (moist tart topped with nuts).

7. Bar Cubano, Andratx
📍 B4 🏠 Plaça Pou, 1
📞 971 136367
This bar is where the locals hang out, and it's filled with the usual gambling machines and Mallorcan pottery.

8. Fet a Sóller, Sóller
📍 C2 🏠 Plaça des Mercat, s/n
📞 971 638839
The name means "Made in Sóller" and that is exactly what you get at this gourmet grocery store: locally made jams and marmalades, olive oils, charcuterie, beers, wine, fresh oranges and much more.

9. Café Sóller, Sóller
📍 V2 🏠 Plaça Constitució, 13
🌐 cafesoller.com
Enjoy modern Mediterranean cuisine at this elegant café. It offers a good mix of vegetarian and meat options.

10. Colmado Sa Lluna, Sóller
📍 C2 🏠 C/Sa Lluna, 3 📞 971 630229
Known locally as a mini Fortnum & Mason, this treasure trove offers wonderful Mallorcan wines and foods, as well as great gift ideas.

Nightclubs and Bars

Pretty entrance to
Aromas, Valldemossa

1. Tim's, Port d'Andratx
A4 Avda. Almirant Riera
Alemany **W** tims.es
A local institution overlooking the
port, Tim's buzzes late into the night.
There is live music at weekends and
screens for watching sports. The
kitchen offers burgers, toasties
and other bar fare.

2. Casino Mallorca, Porto Pi, Palma
C4 Porto Pi Centro Commercial,
Avda. Gabriel Roca, 54 **971 13000**
Fix your eyes on the gaming tables
here and it's easy to imagine you are
in Las Vegas. There is also a glitzy
cocktail bar for a drink between bets.

3. Scubar, Santa Ponça
B4 Via Creu, 15 **600 637782**
With blue-and-white decor, this
friendly beach bar is an exceptionally
relaxed spot to enjoy a post-beach
cocktail. It also does simple but tasty
snacks, and there are live music
performances once a week.

4. Café Sa Plaça, Fornalutx
D2 Plaça Espanya, 4 **871 872187**
This is the most popular of the village-
square bars, and it is open until late in
the summer serving delicious tapas,
pizza, pasta and cocktails.

5. Aromas, Valldemossa
C3 C/Rosa, 24 **971 612341**
The plant-filled patio at this charming
café is the perfect spot to relax with a
glass of wine or a cocktail and a platter
of cheeses and charcuterie.

6. Café Central, Sóller
W2 Plaça Constitució, 32
W cafecentralsoller.com
A popular café that gets really busy
at dawn. A good place to have some
late tapas and a cocktail or two.

7. Port de Nuit Music Bar, Port de Sóller
C2 Passeig Es Traves, 23
699 092000
Enjoy cocktails at this beachfront
bar. It hosts DJ sessions and live
music during summer months.

8. Es Mirall, Port de Sóller
C2 Camí d'es Far, 21
W esmirall.com
With a terrace overlooking the bay,
this lively bar offers karaoke nights
and live music performances.

9. Bar Albatros, Port de Sóller
C2 C/Marina, 48 **W** albatros
portdesoller.com
Soak up the lovely views over the port
while enjoying the excellent paella at
this bar, which is popular with both
visitors and locals alike.

10. Kokomo Surf Café, Cala Major
C4 C/Guillem Díaz-Plaja, 3
W kokomocalamayor.com
Set right on Cala Major beach,
this casual bar has an extensive
all-day menu and great sea views.

Places to Eat

1. Es Turó, Fornalutx
D2 ⌂ Avda. Arbona Colom, 12
☎ 971 630808 ⏱ Thu · €
This family-run mountain restaurant serves delicious suckling pig and other home-cooked Mallorcan favourites.

2. Es Fum, Costa d'en Blanes
C4 ⌂ C/Palma-Andratx, 19, Costa d'en Blanes ⏱ Nov–Mar
ⓦ restaurant-esfum.com · €€€
This great restaurant has a prime location and is set within one of Mallorca's most agreeable resorts.

3. Sebastian, Deià
C2 ⌂ C/Felipe Bauzá, Deià ⏱ L & Wed ⓦ restaurantesebastian.com · €€€
Deià is something of a magnet for celebrities, and this restaurant, serving Mediterranean cuisine, is one of their favourite haunts.

4. Meson Ca'n Pedro, Genova
C4 ⌂ Rector Vives, 4 ⓦ canpedro. es · €€
This hugely popular place with a friendly vibe has been run by the same family since 1976. It offers a wide choice of Mallorcan dishes, but is famed for its succulent grilled meats.

5. Agapanto, Port de Sóller
C2 ⌂ C/Camino del Faro, 2 ⏱ Wed ⓦ agapanto.com · €€€
Mediterranean food, offered up in a classy environment with great views.

Lovely view from Agapanto, Port de Sóller

PRICE CATEGORIES
For a three-course meal for one with half a bottle of wine (or equivalent meal), taxes and extra charges.

€ under €30 €€ €30–50 €€€ over €50

6. Sa Clastra, Es Capdellà
B4 ⌂ Castell Son Claret, Ctra Es Capdellà–Galilea, km 1.7 ⏱ Nov–Feb
ⓦ castellsonclaret.com · €€€
Headed by talented Mallorcan chef Jordi Cantó, this five-star hotel offers a dining experience that infuses traditional island flavours with innovative gastronomy.

7. Bens d'Avall, Deià
C2 ⌂ Urb. Costa Deià, Ctra Sóller Deià, s/n ⏱ Nov–Feb ⓦ bensdavall. com · €€€
A popular restaurant with stunning mountain and sea views, and Mediterranean and nouvelle cuisine. The menu changes each month to make the most of the season's best produce.

8. Es Canyís, Port de Sóller
C2 ⌂ Passeig Platja d'en Repic, 21 ⏱ Mon & Tue ⓦ escanyis.es · €€
Overlooking the seafront, this elegant, family-run restaurant has been serving fresh seafood and local dishes for more than half a century. Save room for the homemade desserts.

9. Ca N'Antuna, Fornalutx
D2 ⌂ C/Arbona Colon, 14
☎ 971 633068 ⏱ Mon · €€
Tasty Mallorcan food, with stunning views from the terrace. The paella is also recommended.

10. Yara Portals, Portals Nous
C4 ⌂ Puerto Portals, Local 1 ⏱ L
ⓦ yarapuertoportals.com · €€€
This waterfront restaurant offers modern Japanese-Mediterranean cuisine. Book a table on the terrace for great harbour views.

Clockwise from above
**Clifftop houses
at sunset near
Valldemossa;
interior of the Real
Cartuja monastery
in Valldemossa;
colourful flowers
outside a building**

NORTH COAST

The north coast of Mallorca is ruggedly beautiful, with a series of jagged peaks rising high above plunging valleys and steep ravines. For the most part, the mountains shield the ocean, but here and there the coast is interrupted by narrow cove beaches and a string of exceptionally pretty mountain villages. The sheer beauty of the landscape has lately attracted a growing number of international visitors, though the British have been coming here in large numbers for many years.

1 Gorg Blau
D2

Heading out of Sóller, on the way to Lluc, the MA-10 is perhaps the most dramatic drive of all, traversing tunnels and narrow gorges on its way between Puig Major and Puig Massanella. This beautiful but bleak ravine has been known since ancient times, as evidenced by the Talayot pillar that has been left as a silent sentinel. Several picturesque reservoirs have been created nearby.

2 Península de Formentor
Mallorca's wildest part *(p40)* is full of vivid vistas and precipitous plunges, where driving or hiking are exhilarating and unforgettable experiences. It is also home to

Observation deck at Península de Formentor

Mallorca's most venerable hotel, where movie stars have stayed, and where crowned heads and diplomats have decided the fate of nations.

3 Son Real
F3 **Ctra Artà–Port d'Alcúdia, km 17** **971 185363**

A combination of working farm, nature reserve and necropolis, the Son Real estate covers almost 4 sq km (1.5 sq miles). The site has had settlements on it since prehistoric times, as the cemetery attests, and today the old restored farm buildings display traditional tools and interiors, and an information centre provides an overview of the area's history. Surrounding the estate is a beautiful nature reserve that is popular with bird-watchers and hikers.

4 Santuari de Lluc
Long before the existence of Christianity, this spot *(p38)* was Mallorca's holiest pilgrimage point. The heady mountain air and the presence of many groves of oak trees, considered sacred in Neolithic and ancient cultures, combine to create a peaceful, inviting atmosphere for believers and non-believers alike. Visitors can arrange to stay in the monastery's comfortable rooms and can explore the many ancient mysteries of the surrounding area.

Statue of a religious figure at the Santuari de Lluc

MALLORCA'S HEIGHTS

The Serra de Tramuntana range runs for 88 km (55 miles) from Andratx in the south to Pollença. Its highest peaks, between Sóller and Lluc, are Puig Major (1,447 m/4,747 ft) and Puig Massanella (1,367 m/4,485 ft). Explore the mountains on foot, if possible, to smell wild rosemary, listen to sheep bells, breathe in pure air and marvel at pine trees.

5 Alcúdia and Port d'Alcúdia

This two-part municipality consists of Mallorca's most striking medieval town (*p44*), uneasily conjoined with one of its brashest tourist ports. The area around the fishing harbour is the most attractive, with the broad promenade of Passeig Marítim facing a row of shops and some excellent fish restaurants.

6 Cala Sant Vicenç
E1

The resort has possibly the clearest, most beautiful blue waters of any truly sandy beach on the island, yet is rarely overcrowded. There are actually three *calas* (coves), Cala Sant Vicenç, Cala Barques and Cala Molins, separated by the Punta de Torre rocky outcrop. Cala Molins is accessed down a steep hill from the main part of the resort and has the most laid-back character, as well as a broader beach and better facilities than the others.

7 Port de Pollença
E1

This port is a major resort with beautiful restaurants, unique shops, a lovely pedestrian-only zone right along the water and bags of nightlife. It is a favourite with families year-round, while older visitors flock here during the winter months. A large community of foreign residents has made Port de Pollença their home.

8 Parc Natural de S'Albufera
F2

The wetland south of Port d'Alcúdia was once a swamp, most of which was drained in the 1860s. The remaining marshes, overgrown with reeds, can be explored via marked trails. A major conservation project, this is an excellent place for bird-watching.

9 Pollença
E1

Founded by the Romans in the foothills of the Serra de Tramuntana, Pollença still has much of its old-world charm with narrow, twisting streets, some good restaurants and a lively Sunday market. There is a great municipal

museum too, while the pride of the town is the beautiful Way of the Cross, leading to a chapel that houses a Gothic statue of Christ. There is a seemingly endless set of steps (365 in all) that climb past the Stations of the Cross, leading to the chapel. The statue is carried around town on Good Friday, in a moving torchlit procession.

10 Santuari de la Mare de Déu del Puig

☐ E2

As with all of Mallorca's religious retreats, it is the serenity of ageless isolation that rewards visitors here. Though located only a 1-hour walk from atmospheric Pollença, this hermitage feels a world away from modern life, set on a modest bump of a hill barely 300 m (984 ft) high. Over the centuries, the typically tawny-hued stone complex has been home to both nuns and monks, but now, even though it is still church property, only overnight guests use the cubicles. A dry-stone path leads up the hill, the air filled with the pungent smell of wild herbs. The arid landscape is broken up with olive, carob and fig trees, and dashes of oleander and wild flowers.

Sunseekers at Cala Molins, Cala Sant Vicenç

A STROLL AROUND POLLENÇA

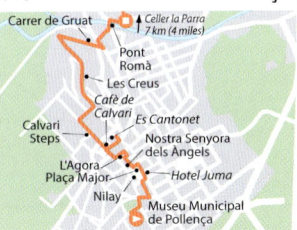

Mid-Morning

This walk around Pollença should take three to four hours.

Start on the southern side of town, with a visit to the **Museu de Pollença** (p61) and the beautiful building that houses it – the convent, church and cloister of Sant Domingo are now given over to civic cultural purposes (closed Mon).

Walk north a couple of blocks and continue up to the **Plaça Major** and admire the Modernista architecture of the **Hotel Juma** and the marvellous rose window tracery of **Nostra Senyora dels Àngels** (p55) parish church. Nearby store **Nilay** (nilay.es), selling handmade fashion items, is worth a visit.

Afternoon

Now walk up the left-hand side of the church along Carrer Monti-Sion and right along Carrer de Joan Mas to **L'Agora** (p117), a shop selling handicrafts. Heading back along Carrer d'Antoni Maura, stop at **Cafè de Calvari** (restaurantcalvaricorner. com) for some refreshments before striding up the **Calvari steps**.

Finally, head down Les Creus and Gruat streets to **Pont Romà**, a bridge thought by some to be from ancient Roman times, but probably dating from the Middle Ages.

Finish the stroll with lunch at **Es Cantonet** (p127) or the popular **Celler la Parra** (p119).

The Best of the Rest

**Cyclists on a road
leading to Puig Major**

1. Mirador de Ses Barques
⊙ C2

Located above Sóller, on the road to Sa Calobra, this marvellous viewpoint overlooks the skein of road loops and, beyond all of the rocky outcroppings, the sea. Stop for refreshment at the restaurant here.

2. Sa Calobra

A rapturously beautiful bay (p74), which explains why the tourist buses pour in by the dozen every day. The drive via the steep, winding road is also memorable. An easier approach is by boat from Port de Sóller, passing isolated bays and with great views of Puig Major.

3. Torrent de Pareis
⊙ D2

There is a walk through a tunnel from Sa Calobra to reach the Torrent de Pareis, which begins in the mountains at the confluence of the torrents of Lluc and Gorg. This canyon is the second largest in the Mediterranean, and the point at which it emerges into the sea is spectacular. However, hiking in the canyon can be dangerous, especially after rain.

4. Puig Major
⊙ D2

Jutting skyward like an enormous stony crown, this majestic mountain rises up from the landscape. It is flanked on one side by the Sóller Valley, with its picturesque villages, and on the other by Lluc (p38) and the tranquil valley of Aubarca.

5. Castell del Rei
⊙ E1

A popular walk leads to this remote, abandoned mountain castle north of Pollença. Please note you need permission (ajpollenca.net/ca) to access the castle complex.

6. Cala Tuent
⊙ D2

A small cove with 13th-century church Ermita de Sant Llorenç (p52), Cala Tuent is probably the quietest beach on the north coast.

7. Santuari Ermita de la Victòria
⊙ F1

Built in 1678, the church is as much a fortress as a spiritual centre due to pirate raids in that era. It houses a revered icon and a vibrant altarpiece.

8. Cap des Pinar
⊙ F1

Much of the cape is a restricted military zone, but you can take in the view from the terrace of the Mirador del Victòria, walk to the ruins of the Talaia d'Alcúdia or climb Penya Roja.

9. Coves de Campanet
⊙ E2 **⊞** C713, 16 km (10 miles) SW of Alcúdia **Ⓦ** covesdecampanet.com

The tour of this cave complex with a lake lasts 45 minutes and is less crowded than others. Visitors can also use the audio guide to take a self-guided tour.

10. Mirador de Mal Pas
⊙ F1

This viewpoint is the first stop on the Península de Formentor (p40).

Cafés and Shops

1. Pinseria Ocho 1907, Pollença
📍 E1 🏠 Plaça Major, 9 📞 971 531598
Overlooking the main square, this is a popular place for a drink. The menu features Italian cuisine – try the crispy pizza-style *pinsas*.

2. Bar Mallorca, Cala Sant Vicenç
📍 E1 🏠 Cala Molins 📞 971 534603
This lovely red-tiled hut overlooking the beach serves a menu of tapas, grilled seafood and traditional Mallorcan dishes.

3. Multi-Hire, Pollença
📍 E1 📍 C/Mendéz Nuñéz, 21
🌐 multi-hire.com
This place offers everything visitors may need to rent on holiday, including bikes for all ages, mobility scooters, baby equipment and air-conditioning units. Food hampers can also be delivered to your accommodation.

4. L'Agora, Pollença
📍 E1 🏠 C/de Joan Mas, 7
📞 616 382022
If you're looking for gifts, make sure to visit this charming shop. It stocks unique Mediterranean-themed ceramics made by local artisans.

5. Rustic Café, Port de Pollença
📍 E1 🏠 Ctra Formentor, 114
📞 640 559591
A café-bar overlooking the seafront, this place has an eclectic menu featuring everything from classic Spanish tapas to Indian samosas and curries. It is part of the popular Pollença tapas route.

6. Teixits Vicens, Pollença
📍 E1 🏠 Can Berenguer Roundabout (Rotonda) 🌐 teixitsvicens.com
Two large floors full of Mallorcan crafts and original art with traditional *robes de llengües* cloth, antiques, lamps, sculpture, rustic furniture, bowls, ceramics and glassware.

7. Helados Garrido, Alcúdia
📍 F2 🏠 C/del Moll 27 📞 971 546931
Set just inside the city walls, this café offers a range of ice-cream flavours to choose from, along with great coffee.

8. U Plaça, Pollença
📍 E1 🏠 Plaça Major, 4 🌐 uplaca.com
Tuck into tasty local tapas, including fried calamari or freshly grilled squid, out on the terrace, which enjoys a prime position on the main square.

9. Arrels, Port de Pollença
📍 E1 🏠 Passeig Saralegui, 54
📞 971 867017
Some of the island's best handmade Mallorcan crafts are stocked here. The traditional ceramic whistles are featured, as well as fine olive-wood carvings and a special line of leather masks by Calimba of Palma.

10. Pizzería de Sa Plaça, Alcúdia
📍 F2 🏠 Plaça de la Constitució
📞 971 548793 🕐 Jan–Mar
A rustic place with a shady terrace overlooking the square, this restaurant serves delicious homemade pizzas and pastas along with coffee and cake.

Wide range of ceramics at Arrels, Port de Pollença

Acrobat show at the Banana Club, Port d'Alcúdia

Nightclubs and Bars

1. La Birreria, Pollença
📍 E1 🏠 C/Temple, 7 📞 657 069850
A veritable temple to beers, this bar
has a local and international range
of artisan beers, including a guest
selection that changes each week.
They also offer delicious tapas.

2. Tecun, Port de Pollença
📍 E1 🏠 C/Ecònom Torres, 11
📞 971 583618
Just a few steps from the marina,
this popular bar hosts regular live
music shows. Enjoy excellent tapas
and cocktails here.

3. Charly's, Can Picafort
📍 F2 🏠 C/Playa, 4 🌐 charlys
canpicafort.com
One of the north coast's
favourite – and longest-running –
nightspots, this club plays soul,
reggae, blues, funk, rock and
alternative music. It also has a
Western-themed saloon bar
and an American dive bar.

4. Skau Disco, Can Picafort
📍 F2 🏠 Avda. José Trias, 14
📞 971 850040 🕒 Winter: Mon–Fri
One of the oldest discos in Mallorca,
Skau was founded in the 1960s. It
is famous for its foam parties.

5. Chivas, Port de Pollença
📍 E1 🏠 C/Metge Llopis, 5 📞 971
864820 🕒 Nov–Apr: Sun–Thu ♿
The crowd is young, and the place
is loud and dark, featuring mirrors
and a glass ceiling with a state-of-
the-art lighting system.

6. The Lemon Lounge, Port de Pollença
📍 E1 🏠 Passeig d'Anglada
Camarasa, 27 📞 971 866250
This elegant, open-air bar is a great
place to relax with a cocktail. There
is also live music in the evenings.

7. Bell's Disco & Club, Port d'Alcúdia
📍 F2 🏠 C/de l'Astoria 📞 602 523507
Open since 1984, this popular late-night
disco-bar plays a mix of latino tunes,
including salsa, bachata and reggae-
ton. There's also a cocktail bar.

8. Enjoy Club, Port d'Alcúdia
📍 F2 🏠 Avda. Tucà, 1 🕒 5pm–
5:30am daily
One of the town's hottest nightspots,
this colourfully lit bar offers innovative
cocktails and live DJ sessions. There's
a lovely outdoor terrace too.

9. Shamrock, Port d'Alcúdia
📍 F2 🏠 C/Torreta, 3 📞 600 348377
A busy Irish pub located in the port,
Shamrock holds varied live music
events every night, and is also a
good place to watch sports on TV.

10. Banana Club, Port d'Alcúdia
📍 F2 🏠 Avda. Tucan, 1 🌐 banana
club.es
Topped with an unmissable glass
pyramid, this is one of the most popular clubs on Mallorca's northern coast.
It attracts locals and tourists thanks to
its great line-up of resident and guest
DJs, and it hosts a number of different
theme nights (including foam parties).

Places to Eat

1. Stay, Port de Pollença
⚲ E1 ⌂ Moll Nou, s/n ⓦ stay
restaurant.com · €€

Fish is the speciality at this excellent upmarket restaurant, but the menu of international fare is huge. The lunch menu is great value.

2. Bella Verde, Port de Pollença
⚲ E1 ⌂ C/Monges, 14 ☎ 675 602528
🚫 Mon · €€

This outstanding vegetarian and vegan restaurant has a lovely shaded courtyard and a superb menu. Dishes include a delicious pumpkin lasagne.

3. Como en Casa, Port d'Alcúdia
⚲ F2 ⌂ C/dels Pins, 4
☎ 971 549033 🚫 Mon, L · €€

Try the fresh, homemade salads on offer at this restaurant.

4. Pollentia Mar, Pollença
⚲ E1 ⌂ Via Pollentia, 19
☎ 971 530632 🚫 D Sun–Thu · €

A wonderful seafood restaurant that specializes in traditional cuisine.

5. Il Giardino, Pollença
⚲ E1 ⌂ Plaça Major, 11
ⓦ ilgiardino.es · €€

One of Pollença's best restaurants, this bistro offers delicious Italian dishes made with fresh, locally sourced produce.

Bright interior of Stay, Port de Pollença

PRICE CATEGORIES

For a three-course meal for one with half a bottle of wine (or equivalent meal), taxes and extra charges.

€ under €30 €€ €30–50 €€€ over €50

---

6. The Hideaway, Port de Pollença
⚲ E1 ⌂ C/Club Sol-Puerto, 13
☎ 636 015052 · €

Tucked away in the Club del Sol resort, this family-run restaurant has an impressive menu that offers Mediterranean fare with a focus on fresh seafood.

7. Q11, Pollença
⚲ E1 ⌂ C/d'Antoni Maura, 11
ⓦ q11restaurant.com · €

Enjoy modern Mediterranean cuisine in a wonderful setting at this restaurant. Vegetarian options are also available.

8. Celler la Parra, Port de Pollença
⚲ E1 ⌂ C/Joan XXIII, 84 🚫 Mon
ⓦ cellerlaparra.com · €€€

A welcoming, traditionally decorated restaurant that is a reminder of quieter island times. The food and wine served here is really first-rate.

9. Miramar, Port d'Alcúdia
⚲ F2 ⌂ Passeig Marítim, 2
ⓦ restaurantmiramar.es · €€

You are spoiled for choice when it comes to great restaurants in Port d'Alcúdia, but this spot is one of the best. The speciality is seafood, but there is a good range of Mediterranean dishes to suit most tastes.

10. Blue Marine, Can Picafort
⚲ F2 ⌂ C/Enginyer Felicià Fuster, 38
☎ 667 680330 · €€

Set at the south end of town and overlooking the marina, this cosy spot is known for its reasonably priced and top-notch seafood.

SOUTHEAST COAST

Mallorca's sun-kissed southeast coast may feature numerous beaches, coves and bays, but it has often been overlooked by tourists who favour the more built-up areas around Palma and the southwest. While some of the local beaches have seen the worst of the effects of mass tourism, more remain pristine and as beautiful as ever, offering some of the Mediterranean's most clear and inviting waters. Here, too, is the verdant Serra de Llevant mountain range and some of the island's best natural parks, not to mention its most important ancient sites and spectacular caves all just waiting to be explored. If your ideal trip to Mallorca includes relaxing on the sands or spending time in the great outdoors, the southeast coast region is for you.

For places to stay in this area, see p146

Medieval market fair at Castell de Capdepera

1 Capdepera

📍 H3

Towering above the town, this castle can be seen from miles away, its crenellated form sprawling appealingly around the crest of its sizable hill. A citadel of some sort has existed here since Roman times, guarding the sea approach from the east, but the present crenellated classic dates back to King Sanç in the 14th century. It is possible to drive up, though it can be difficult to find the right street in the tightly knit little town below. The walk up from pleasant Plaça de l'Orient is a much better option. Within the walls is a curious little Gothic church that offers spectacular views of the town's terracotta roofscape from its flat roof.

2 Coves d'Artà

📍 H3 🏠 Ctra de las Coves, Capdepera ⏰ 10am–5pm daily 🌐 cuevasdearta.com 📷📷

During the Christian Conquest, Jaume I found 2,000 Moors hiding with their cattle in this unusual network of caves. However, it was not until 1876, when speleologist Édouard Martel entered the grottoes, 46 m (151 ft) above the sea at Cap Vermell, that they were studied. Another early visitor was Jules Verne, whose book *Journey to the Centre of the Earth* is said to have been inspired by them.

3 Ses Països

📍 G3 🏠 South of Artà ⏰ Apr–Oct: 10am–5pm Mon–Fri, 10am–2pm Sat 📷

A link with the Mallorcans of some 3,000 years ago, these Bronze Age ruins of a Talayot village (*p8*) include a massive Cyclopean portal formed from three stone slabs weighing up to eight tons each. Inside are several rooms and a watchtower, and the settlement is surrounded by a dry-stone wall.

4 Coves del Drac

Mallorca's most spectacular cave system (*p46*) can be toured in a gondola-style boat. The experience is enhanced by live music.

Underground lake at the Coves del Drac

Relaxing on the beach, Parc Natural de Mondragó

5 Illa de Cabrera

Cabrera ("Goat Island") lies 18 km (11 miles) off the mainland. A rocky place and virtually uninhabited, it nevertheless has a rich history. It served as a prison camp during the Napoleonic Wars and was used as a base by Barbary pirates. Since 1991, Cabrera has been part of the archipelago's marine national park *(p30)*, and is the only visitable island. This protection extends not only to rare species of plants, but also includes the surrounding marine life. Boat trips *(excursionsacabrera.es)* leave from Colònia de Sant Jordi daily and take a day – highlights include a 14th-century castle *(p30)* on the island and the Cova Blava *(p30)* grotto.

SUSTAINABLE TOURISM

The 1960s mass tourism left its mark on Mallorca's environment. "Eco-tax" was introduced in 2016, which led to increased investment in protecting Mallorca's natural environments, and has enabled a more sustainable tourism infrastructure to be built.

Keep an eye out for the rare Eleonora's Falcon and Lilford's lizard, the latter identifiable by its dog-like face.

6 Parc Natural de Mondragó
F6 **South of Portopetro**

Marked as a protected area in 1992, the park incorporates dunes, marshes, rocky coasts, beaches, pine forest, farmland and scrub. Country lanes and easy trails provide access. Look out for herons, egrets, puffins, coots, finches and rabbits. The park's visitor information centre is next to the Ses Fonts den'Alis car park.

7 Cala Figuera
F6

This tiny old fishing hamlet is an underdeveloped gem. It probably owes its survival to the simple fact that it has no beach, the closest one being 4 km (2 miles) away at Cala Santanyí. There is a collection of pleasant low-rise structures and an array of restaurants. The fishing harbour is part of a fjordlike bay.

8 Coves d'es Hams

These caves *(p47)* are less striking than the Coves del Drac or Coves d'Artà. The name Hams means "fish-hooks", which the stalactites are said to resemble. Visitors get a guided tour and a concert.

9 Capocorb Vell
⊙ D5 **⌂** Ctra MA–6014 Llucmajor–Cap Blanc, km 23 **☎** 971 180155 **⊙** 10am–5pm Fri–Wed

This Talayot settlement was probably established around 1000 BCE. Originally, it consisted of five stone structures (talayots) and 28 smaller dwellings. The Cyclopean walls would have served as protection, but little more is known about the function of the rooms or the lives of the ancient inhabitants. Part of the charm here lies in its setting among fields of fruit trees and dry-stone walls. Have a drink at the visitors' bar, which would not look out of place in *The Flintstones*. Apart from the snack bar, the site remains undeveloped and peaceful.

10 Santuari de Sant Salvador
⊙ F5 **⌂** Ctra de Portocolon, s/n, Felanitx **☎** 971 515260

The castle-like structure is 4 km (2 miles) east of Felanitx, on Puig Sant Salvador, the highest mountain of the Serra de Llevant. Founded in the 14th century, and remodelled in the 18th century, the sanctuary is an important place of pilgrimage. As in other former monasteries, visitors can stay in basic rooms.

Creu des Picot stone cross, Santuari de Sant Salvador

FIVE SEASIDE BEAUTIES

Morning
This itinerary, with driving and walking, will take a full day.

Set out in the morning to lovely **Porto Cristo** *(p124)*, with its terrace café-restaurants that look over the picturesque port. Pop into the local boutique and enjoy a coffee at **Claudia's Café** *(p125)*.

Bypassing the overdeveloped Cales de Mallorca, **Portocolom** *(p124)* is next, perhaps the most unspoiled and beautiful fishing village left on the island. Be sure to check out the painted façades of the Old Town, and walk along the waterfront to **Restaurant Club Nàutic** *(p127)* for a delicious seafood lunch while enjoying the stunning views over the harbour.

Afternoon
Make your way down to pretty **Portopetro** *(p65)*, a minuscule port that has lost none of its historic charm. Have a drink at **Ca'n Martina** *(p127)*, a restaurant that is in a beautiful setting overlooking the bay.

Picturesque **Cala Figuera** is further south. Stroll around its woods-encircled harbour and browse around the gift shops.

On the western side of the Cap de ses Salines is Colònia de Sant Jordi, a beach town with a port. Stop here to have a fish dinner at **Port Blau** *(p127)*, and spend the night at **Hostal Playa** *(p146)*.

The Best of the Rest

Colourful houses lining the harbour, Portocolom

1. Artà
📍 G3

An ancient, prosperous town, Artà is best known for its basketry.

2. Cala Ratjada
📍 H3

Surrounded by fine beaches and pretty coves, this fishing port on Mallorca's eastern tip is a busy resort in summer.

3. Santanyí
📍 F6

This is the café centre for all the expats who own villas nearby, but it is still very Spanish. Buildings are made from the same golden sandstone used in Palma's Cathedral. The streets near the church are the focus of a lively Wednesday market.

4. Porto Cristo
📍 G4

Located at the end of a sheltered inlet, Porto Cristo is a family resort. The nearby Coves del Drac and Coves d'es Hams (p47) are especially popular with daytrippers.

5. Portocolom
📍 G5

This attractive fishing village was named after Christopher Columbus, who is said to have been born here. It has found a new lease of life as a resort favoured by the Spanish.

6. Felanitx
📍 F5

The town is at the centre of a wine-producing area and also known for its floral-decorated pottery and its capers, or "green pearls", which are on sale at the Sunday market.

7. Cala d'Or
📍 F5

Many coves – each with their respective beaches and pueblo-style villas – make up this stylish area. Each former humble fishing dock has metamorphosed into a classy marina.

8. Castell de Santuari
📍 G3

Artà's crowning glory is its hilltop fortress, the view from which is Mallorca's most characteristic sight: a jumble of tiles in every shade of brown.

9. Campos
📍 E5

A famous painting by 17th-century Sevillian artist Murillo hangs in the parish church of this dusty agricultural town. Next door is a museum with a collection of offertory bowls.

10. Ses Covetes
📍 E6

There is no trace of the "small caves", presumed ancient Roman burial niches, that inspired the name of this town. Located at the northern end of Es Trenc (p68), this place has a great beach and a few cafés.

Wickerwork at the Santanyí market

Cafés and Shops

1. Café del Mar, Cala Ratjada
◉ H3 ⌂ C/Castellet ☎ 693 450849
Set on a prime spot overlooking the water, this Mediterranean café serves healthy breakfasts prepared with fresh local produce.

2. Claudia's Café, Porto Cristo
◉ G4 ⌂ C/d'En Bordils, 59
Ⓦ claudias.cafe
Just a few steps from Porto Cristo beach, this sunny café offers croissants and coffee, as well as tapas and cocktails.

3. Café 3, Cala Ratjada
◉ H3 ⌂ Avda. America, 4
☎ 971 565356
With views over the marina, this light and airy bar has balconies and spacious, decked outdoor areas, giving it a beach-house feel. During the summer months, there is live music.

4. Caféteria Chambi, Porto Cristo
◉ G4 ⌂ San Jordi, 2 ☎ 971 820787
Offering modern Mediterranean food, this café has great tapas, as well as a wide variety of vegetarian options.

5. Sa Plaça, Santanyí
◉ F6 ⌂ Plaça Major, 26 Ⓦ saplasa
santanyi.com
Come for *pa amb oli (p83)*, olives, ham, pickled peppers and Mallorcan cheeses. The refurbished interior has marble tabletops and archways, and outside there is plenty of local action in the main square.

6. Mandala Shoes, Santanyí
◉ F6 ⌂ C/Bisbe Verger, 34 ◷ 10:30am–2pm & 4:30–8pm Mon–Fri, 10am–3pm Sat Ⓦ mandalashoes.com
An exclusive shop for quality leather shoes. Golf shoes are a speciality here. Tailor-made products also available.

7. Artesania Son Pocapalla, Artà
◉ G3 ⌂ Plaça del Conqueridor, 10
Ⓦ sonpocapalla.com

Artà town is famous for everyday items made from the tough fibres of the *palmito* (palmetto) plant, which grows wild all over the island. Shop for baskets, hats and homeware here.

8. Panaderia Pons, Colònia de Sant Jordi
◉ E6 ⌂ C/Major, 20 Ⓦ panaderia
pons.com
The *ensaimades* (spiral-shaped sweet pastries) from here are light and fluffy and are sold alongside other delicious local pastries and various picnic essentials.

9. Cafe Val, Santanyí
◉ F6 ⌂ Plaça Major, 28 ◷ Sun
Ⓦ cafe-val.com
With beamed ceilings and exposed brick walls, this café offers good breakfasts and international cuisine. There is also a patio and a roof terrace for alfresco meals.

10. Annagramma, Santanyí
◉ F6 ⌂ Plaça de la Constitució, 4
Ⓦ annagramma.com
A fashion boutique offering a range of women's clothing that blends Eastern influences with Italian style.

Rocky coastline at the seaside resort of Cala Ratjada

Nightclubs and Bars

1. Physical, Cala Ratjada
📍 H3 🏠 C/de Xuclamel 📞 669 382977
The port attracts a young, active crowd for whom this is the best club in town, leading the way with techno, hip-hop and dance music.

2. Twist, Porto Cristo
📍 G4 🏠 Es Riuet 📞 971 820173
A hip place done up in primary colours, with tiny halogen lights above a granite bar and work by Basque artist S'Anto Iñorrieta.

3. Flamingo, Porto Cristo
📍 G4 🏠 C/Bordils 📞 971 822259
Offering delicious homemade paellas and seafood, this bar and restaurant has an unusual decor that includes cartoons on the walls. Outside, the views from the terrace are superb.

4. Noah's Lounge, Cala Ratjada
📍 H3 🏠 Avda. América, 1–2
🌐 cafenoahs.com
Located on the harbour, with pretty views, this laid-back spot serves healthy food from early in the morning, and cocktails until late at night. Full access for guests with limited mobility.

5. Café Chill Out La Playa, Portocolom
📍 G5 🏠 C/del Corb Marí, 14 🌐 cafe-chill-out-la-playa.makro.bar
A cool and relaxing terrace-bar by the beach with, as the name suggests, a chilled-out vibe. International DJs play Nu Jazz here most evenings.

6. Bolero Angels Disco, Cala Ratjada
📍 H3 🏠 C/Leonor Servera, 36
🌐 bolero-angels.com
This glamorously appointed disco is right in the heart of Cala Ratjada. DJs play pop and dance music to the young crowd, and there is live music most nights of the week as well.

7. Cala Gran Cocktail Bar, Santanyí
📍 F6 🏠 C/Blvd d'Or, 4 📞 663 027605
Located in the centre of town, this welcoming cocktail bar has great drinks and an amazing terrace. It offers full access to visitors with limited mobility.

8. Café Parisien, Artà
📍 G3 🏠 C/Ciutat, 18 📞 971 835440
An artistic café with a vintage air and a beautiful garden terrace, Café Parisien is an institution in Artà. It serves snacks and modern seasonal cuisine.

9. The Beach Bar, S'Illot
📍 G4 🏠 Rda. del Mati, 9 📞 871 539056
This colourful bar serves up delicious fresh fruit mojitos, daiquiris and reasonably priced food on its beach-front terrace. More relaxed by day, it gets livelier on summer evenings.

10. Carpe Diem, Portopetro
📍 F6 🏠 Passeig des Port, 52
Live music and a breezy terrace make this bar a great place to spend the hot summer nights. Drop in for coffee and cakes during the day.

Outdoor tables at Cala Gran
Cocktail Bar, Santanyí

Places to Eat

Waterfront setting at Ca'n Martina, Portopetro

1. S'Assecador, Porto Cristo
📍 G4 🏠 C/Mar, 11 ☎ 971 820826 · €€

Enjoy a view of the marina while you tuck into a traditional Mallorcan meal at this restaurant decorated with Moroccan tilework.

2. Restaurant Principal, Manacor
📍 F4 🏠 Hotel Son Amoixa Vell, Ctra Cales de Mallorca, km 3.4 ☎ 971 846292 🕐 Tue · €€€

A romantic spot with a beautiful terrace, Restaurant Principal offers an à la carte menu featuring seasonal as well as daily recommendations.

3. Sa Cuina, Portocolom
📍 G5 🏠 Ctra S'Horta–Portocolom; C/Vapor de Santueri, s/n ☎ 971 824080 🕐 Thu; Jan · €

The food at Sa Cuina combines traditional Mallorcan dishes and modern international cuisine. The decor is a nice mix of traditional and contemporary.

4. Restaurant Club Nàutic, Portocolom
📍 G5 🏠 C/Pescadors, 31 🕐 Tue 🌐 clubnautic.es · €€

Both locals and tourists are drawn to this waterfront establishment for its delicious seafood and scenic harbour setting.

5. Tomeu Caldentey Cuiner, Sa Coma
📍 G4 🏠 C/Liles 🌐 tomeucaldentey.com · €€€

Michelin-star-winning chef offers creative fixed-price tasting menus at his eponymous restaurant.

6. Es Cantonet, Santanyí
📍 F6 🏠 Plaça Bernareggi, 2 🕐 Sun 🌐 es-cantonet.net · €€

Creative Mediterranean fare served in a historic Mallorcan building.

7. L'Arcada, Cala Figuera
📍 F6 🏠 C/Virgen del Carmen, 80 🌐 restaurantlarcada.com · €€

With the central spot on the port and the best views, L'Arcada serves fresh fish dishes depending on the day's catch.

8. Ses Portadores, Portocolom
📍 G5 🏠 Rda. Miquel Massutí Alzamora, 59 ☎ 971 825271 · €€

Soak in the views of the bay while tucking into Mediterranean dishes, such as fresh seafood and steaks.

9. Port Blau, Colònia de Sant Jordi
📍 E6 🏠 C/Gabriel Roca, 67 🕐 Tue; Jan & Dec 🌐 portblau.es · €€

Uses fish caught around Illa de Cabrera, served up in vast portions in an open dining area on the port.

10. Ca'n Martina, Portopetro
📍 F6 🏠 Passeig des Port ☎ 971 657517 · €€

Come for freshly caught seafood and expertly cooked Mallorcan specialities, including black paella.

CENTRAL PLAIN

A visit to Mallorca is only really complete after an exploration of the vast and mostly flat Es Pla (The Plain). People often argue about whether the mountains or coast better represents the real Mallorca, but the true heart of the island is surely to be found in the villages of this central region, which still to this day make few concessions to tourism. This is the island's workshop – where food is grown and where most of the leather-workers, potters and manufacturers of traditional *robes de llengües* (tongues of flame) and prized artificial pearls are based.

1 Lloseta

D3

Traditionally part of the area's leather-crafting enterprises, this town is situated on a sloping foothill. It has a tree-lined approach, a pretty little central square and several good restaurants offering local cuisine.

2 Inca

E3

One of the many stops on the train journey from Palma to Sa Pobla, Inca is a modern industrial place, but visitors come for the cheap leather goods found in Avinguda General Luque and Gran Via de Colon. Thursday, market

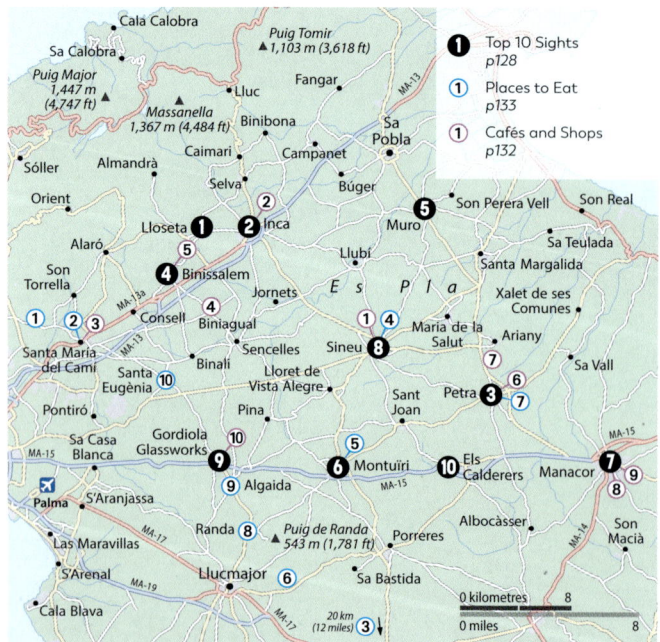

For places to stay in this area, see p147

Colourful wicker baskets on sale, Inca

day, is Inca's busiest time, trading in souvenirs, household goods, flowers and food. The town is also known for its traditional cuisine, including *caracoles* (snails), and its wine cellars turned into restaurants.

3 Petra
F4

This small town is the place of birth of Junípero Serra. At 36 years of age, the pioneering Franciscan monk travelled to America and Mexico and, after many arduous journeys on foot, founded missions in both Los Angeles and San Francisco. The houses lining the narrow alleys have changed little since Serra's time here. The town makes the most of its famous son, and all places associated with Serra are well marked. These include a humble building in Carrer Barracar Alt where he was born. Next to this is a small museum. Opened in 1955 and devoted to his life and work, it includes wooden models of the nine American missions established by Serra. However, there is no reference to his treatment of Native Americans, for which he is today heavily criticized. At the end of the street where the Serra family house stands is the 17th-century monastery of Sant Bernat. Majolica

panels down a side street next to the monastery pay tribute to the monk.

4 Binissalem
D3

Do not be put off by its rather workaday appearance from the highway. Hidden behind commercial enterprises, the historic centre dates back to the ancient Romans, and is now dominated by centuries-old stone mansions that are very much worth a stroll around. The town's wealth arose from its pre-eminence as the island's wine producer, starting in the early 1500s. In recent years, after a century or so of decline, its reputation has again been on the rise, as evidenced by the important vineyard outlets along the main road.

Traditional windmill behind a vineyard, Binissalem

5 Muro
E3

This is a pleasant, sleepy town full of old mansions and dominated by the church of Sant Joan Baptista. The adjacent belfry has wonderful views of the area. The town's Museu Etnológic is also worth a visit, and houses furniture, tools, costumes and instruments.

6 Montuïri
E4

Built on a hill, the town of Montuïri is famous for its agricultural produce. Nineteen of the original twenty-four windmills still stand as testimony to the town's former glory, striking in the landscape. The Ermita de Sant Miquel (p52) is nearby, offering good views and a café-restaurant.

7 Manacor
F4

Mallorca's second city is famous for being the hometown of former world No. 1 tennis champion Rafael Nadal and for artificial pearl factories, of which Perlas Majorica (p132) is the best known. The method of pearl production can be witnessed on the free tour. Also worth a look inside is the Església de Nostra Senyora dels Dolors, where pilgrims line up to kiss the feet of a figure of Christ.

8 Sineu
E3

At the geographical centre of the island, this hilly little town is distinguished by its impressive church, Nostra Senyora dels Àngels, a medieval structure with a bell tower that soars above a huddle of old stone cottages. Nearby is the main square, Sa Plaça, the site of a large farmers' market every Wednesday morning.

> #### MALLORCA'S WINDMILLS
>
> Mallorca is famous for its windmills, especially in the region of Es Pla. These devices have been used in the Mediterranean since the 7th century. Now replaced by motorized pumps, most of the stone windmills have fallen into disrepair. However, in the region between Palma, Algaida and Llucmajor, ecologically minded farmers have renovated their old windmills.

Glass-blower at work,
Gordiola Glassworks

9 Gordiola Glassworks

📍 D4 🏠 Ctra Palma–Manacor,
km 19, Algaida ⏰ 9am–6pm Mon–
Fri, 9am–2pm Sat 🌐 gordiola.com

The glassworks were founded in
1719, but the present castle-like, Neo-
Gothic building dates from the 1960s.
The fascinating place offers visitors
a unique opportunity to watch glass-
blowers at work, and its world-class
museum of glass also fires enthusiasm
for the craft. An on-site shop sells
everything from inexpensive trinkets
to chandeliers fit for a castle.

10 Els Calderers

📍 E4 🏠 Follow signs from
MA-15 ⏰ Apr–Oct: 10am–6pm
daily; Nov–Mar: 10am–5pm daily
🌐 elscalderers.com 🏠🏠

Established in the 17th century
by the Veri family, this country
house chronicles 200 years of local
gentry life. Today, parts of the house,
including the private chapel, the gra-
nary and the large kitchen, are open
to the public. Displays of traditional
methods are part of the tour, and you
can see historic breeds of Mallorcan
farm animals.

Església de Nostra Senyora
dels Dolors, Manacor

A DAY'S DRIVE THROUGH ES PLA

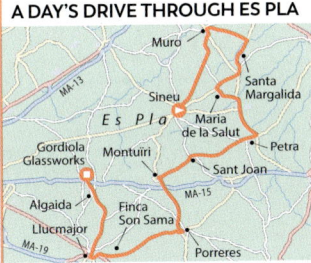

Morning

Begin in the north of Es Pla, at
the medieval town of **Sineu** and
be sure to visit the church of
Nostra Senyora dels Àngels
(p130). Stroll around and stop for
a drink and a snack at **Panord
Forn** (p132). Proceed north to
Muro for a look at the handsome
Sant Joan Baptista church and
the fascinating Museu Etnològic.

Drive on through pretty Santa
Margalida, then Maria de la Salut.

By now, it should be lunchtime, so
continue to **Petra** (p129) to have a
meal at **Can Salom** (p133), and to
check out the hometown of the
missionary Franciscan monk
Junípero Serra (p91).

Afternoon

After lunch, make the way
on through Sant Joan and then
to appealing **Montuïri**, with its
signature windmills. Next, cut
down to Porreres and take the
road from there to Llucmajor. Be
sure to stop off along the way
for a walk around the quaintly
picturesque grounds and gardens
of the **Finca Son Sama** mansion.

The last leg of the journey is to
head back north to **Algaida** (p62),
being sure to pop into Raïms for
a look at its timeless charm.

Finally, just to the west of
Algaida, take a prolonged tour
of the **Gordiola Glassworks**, with
its superb museum and shop.

Cafés and Shops

Jewellery at Perlas Majorica, Manacor

1. Panord Forn, Sineu

📍 E3 🏠 Plaça Es Fossar, 13
🌐 panord.es

This pleasant café-bakery, overlooking Sineu's main square, offers fresh-from-the-oven pastries and coffee.

2. ReCamper, Inca

📍 E3 🏠 C/Cuartel, 91, Poligono Industrial 🌐 camper.com

The famous Spanish brand's shoes are made right here and visitors can have first pick of the newest styles at reduced prices.

3. Artesanía Textil Bujosa, Santa Maria del Camí

📍 D3 🏠 C/Bernardo Santa Eugènia, 53 (E of Bunyola) 🌐 bujosatextil.com

The only manufacturer of *robes de llengües* (tongues of flame cloth) that still uses traditional methods on antique looms. Tablecloths and other furnishings are sold.

4. Bodega Biniagual, Binissalem

📍 D3 🏠 Camí de Muro, 11 🌐 finca-biniagual.com 🔗

The village of Biniagual was restored and now once again produces wine. This bodega has become one of the most prestigious wineries here. Tours and tastings need to be pre-booked.

5. José L Ferrer, Binissalem

📍 D3 🏠 C/Conquistador, 103
🕐 10am–6pm Mon–Sat, 10am–4pm Sun 🌐 vinosferrer.com 🔗

This famous winery is worth a stop for the tour and the wine-tasting. Their reds are made from Mantonegro and Callet grapes, and the white from Moll. Book ahead for wine tastings.

6. Bar Ca'n Tomeu, Petra

📍 F4 🏠 C/Sol, 47 📞 971 561023

By the main square, this bar has a local feel and decor. The menu features *pa amb oli (p83)*, tapas, salads and other more elaborate dishes.

7. Miquel Oliver, Petra

📍 F4 🏠 C/Font, 26 🌐 miqueloliver.com 🔗

Found in the little town of Petra, this bodega has a reputation for great dry white wines. Among many vintages, the Muscat Original is generally regarded as the best pick. Tours must be booked in advance.

8. Perlas Majorica, Manacor

📍 F4 🏠 Vía Palma, 9 📞 971 550900 🔗

This is the island's best-known imitation pearl factory, where the gems are made and then skilfully set into necklaces and bracelets by crafters. Tour the factory and browse the finished pieces in the shop.

9. Art-Metall, Manacor

📍 F4 🏠 Menendez Pelayo, 38
🌐 artmetalldellevant.com

The place to find the wrought-iron objects seen all over the island, such as candelabras and mirrors.

10. Gordiola Glassworks, Algaida

A great collection of glass from around the world, ranging from ancient to modern, with an amazing array of glass merchandise are available here *(p131)*. Some products can also be customized.

Places to Eat

1. Molí des Torrent, Santa Maria del Camí
📍D3 🏠Ctra de Bunyola, 75 🕐Wed & Thu 🌐molidestorrent.de · €€
Set in a restored windmill, Molí des Torrent serves traditional Mallorcan dishes with a German twist. There is also an excellent wine list.

2. Celler Sa Sini, Santa Maria del Camí
📍D3 🏠Plaça Hostals, 20 🕐Mon & Tue 🌐cellersasini.net · €
Cosy and delightfully old-fashioned, this traditional Mallorcan restaurant dishes up local favourites, such as *frit mallorquí (p82)*, and good pizzas.

3. Es Brollador Bar Resturante
📍F6 🏠Plaça Fray Junipero Serra ☎971 830332 🕐Mon · €
Set in a pretty little square with olive and palm trees, this restaurant seres traditional Mallorquín dishes as well as, a variety of pizzas, salads and burgers.

4. La Cocina, Sineu
📍E3 🏠C/Major, 7 ☎621 249709 🕐Mon & Tue · €
Charming restaurant serving top-notch traditional tapas with ham and cheese platters and daily specials.

5. Restaurant Xorri, Montuïri
📍E4 🏠C/Major, 2 🌐canxorri.es · €
A classic country restaurant, this is a good place to sit out on the terrace with some great local food and a glass of wine and soak up the view.

6. Es Mirador, Llucmajor
📍D5 🏠Finca Son Sama, Ctra Llucmajor–Porreres, hm 3.5 ☎971 120959 🕐Sun; mid-Dec–Feb · €€
Enjoy à la carte traditional fare, or sample the tasting menu as you take in the terrific views from the terrace.

Garden at Moli des Torrent, Santa Maria del Camí

PRICE CATEGORIES

For a three-course meal for one with half a bottle of wine (or equivalent meal), taxes and extra charges.

€ under €30 €€ €30–50 €€€ over €50

---

7. Can Salom, Petra
📍F4 🏠Plaça Fray Junípero Serra, 4 🕐Mon 🌐cansalom.com · €
Set in a leafy square, this restaurant serves quality homemade food.

8. Sa Tanqueta de Randa, Algaida
📍D4 🏠C/de sa Tanqueta, 1 🌐satanqueta.com · €€
Enjoy Mallorcan dishes made with local produce here.

9. Restaurant Ca'l Dimoni, Algaida
📍D4 🏠Ctra Manacor, hm 21 ☎971 665035 🕐Wed · €
This restaurant serves dishes such as barbecued lamb and suckling pig.

10. Sa Torre de Santa Eugènia, Santa Eugènia
📍D3 🏠Ctra de Santa Maria a Sencelles 🌐sa-torre.com · €€
This restaurant in the 15th-century cellar of an ancient family house serves delicious Mediterranean food.

STREETSMART

Colourful sign in Valldemossa

GETTING AROUND

Whether exploring Mallorca by foot or making use of public transportation, here is everything you need to know to navigate the city and the surrounding areas like a pro.

AT A GLANCE

PUBLIC TRANSPORT COSTS

BUS

€2.00

Single-ride ticket

METRO

€1.80

Single-ride ticket

TREN DE SÓLLER

€20.00

Single-ride ticket

SPEED LIMIT

MOTORWAYS

120 km/h
(75 mph)

DUAL CARRIAGEWAY

100 km/h
(60 mph)

SECONDARY ROAD

90 km/h
(55 mph)

URBAN AREAS

30 km/h
(20 mph)

Arriving by Air

Scheduled and charter flights connect **Mallorca's Palma Airport** with major Spanish and European cities. There are regular direct flights from Britain, Germany, Austria, France, Switzerland and the Netherlands; visitors from the US or Canada will have to make the connection somewhere in Europe, usually in Madrid. Onward connections to Mallorca can be made with a number of carriers who operate regular flights between mainland Spain and Mallorca. Some carriers also operate flights to Palma from the neighbouring islands of Ibiza and Menorca. If taking one of these routes, it is a good idea to find out what type of aircraft you are going to fly in, as some are quite small and you may not be able to take large hand luggage.

The airport is 11 km (6 miles) southeast of the capital. The nearby motorway provides a fast road link to Palma, with taxis and buses taking visitors to the city and resorts. The **Aena** website displays all bus routes to destinations around the island. The number 1 bus operates regularly between the airport and the transport system in central Palma.

Aena
W aena.es
Palma de Mallorca Airport
W palmaairport.info

Arriving via Land

While there are no land connections to Mallorca itself, it is possible to access the island by travelling across mainland Spain via road or rail, and then catching a ferry for the final leg. These can be boarded at Barcelona, Valencia, Alicante and Dénia.

Spain's international and domestic rail services are operated by state-run **Renfe** (Red Nacional de Ferrocarriles Españoles). For international train trips, it is advisable to purchase your ticket well in advance.

International coach routes operate regular routes between Spain and elsewhere in Europe.
Renfe
🌐 renfe.com

Arriving by Ferry
There are frequent and regular services between several large towns on the Spanish mainland and Mallorca. The island has two ports for passenger traffic: Palma, the main port of the island, and Alcúdia, in the north. The **Trasmediterránea** ferry company operates several routes from Barcelona, Valencia and Alicante to Palma, and **Baleària** sails to Alcúdia from Barcelona and from Dénia to Palma via Ibiza. Journeys take approximately 4–8 hours.

There are also regular ferries between Mallorca and the other Balearic Islands. Baleària operates routes from Alcúdia to Ciutadella in Menorca, and Palma to Ibiza. Trasmediterránea also runs a ferry service from Ibiza and Menorca to Palma. Some routes offer a choice of high-speed and standard ferries: check in advance. Price differences depend mostly on the time of year; the lowest prices are found in low season, from October until the end of March.

In high season, there is a further ferry service to Alcúdia from Toulon in France. This is run by **Corsica Ferries** and has a journey time of around 12 hours.
Baleària
🌐 balearia.com
Corsica Ferries
🌐 corsica-ferries.co.uk
Trasmediterránea
🌐 trasmediterranea.es

Public Transport
Mallorca's public transport network comprises train, bus and metro services. Tickets for all three are managed by **Consorci Transport Mallorca (CTM)**, which has route maps and timetables on its website.
Consorci Transport Mallorca (CTM)
🌐 tib.org

Tickets
The cheapest and most convenient ticket option for public transport is to use a contactless bank card; you just need to ensure that you validate the card when both boarding and alighting the bus, train or metro. The same bank card can be used for groups of up to five people, with a discount on the standard ticket price applied for each additional person. (So a single journey for one person might cost €1.80, but when five people are travelling the price drops to €1.20 each.) Each member of the group must validate the bank card in the usual way. Up to two transfers can be made when travelling on three different lines, as long as they take place within 60 minutes of validating the exit from one line and entering the next. And regardless of how long the total journey is, no more than four transfers will ever be charged.

Those without a contactless bank card can purchase train and metro tickets from the machines inside all stations, and bus tickets (cash only) on board from the driver. Note, however, that tickets purchased this way are generally more expensive, and are also valid for a single journey only – they cannot be used to transfer to other lines.

Train and Tram
There are three regular railway lines on the island operated by **Serveis Ferroviaris de Mallorca (SFM)**, all of which depart from the Intermodal train station located on Palma's Plaça d'Espanya: T1 runs to Inca, T2 to Sa Pobla and T3 (following much of the same route as T2) runs to Manacor.

The privately owned Tren de Sóller has been operating for more than a century and offers special trips from Palma to Sóller, for an extra cost, between April and October. The same company also runs a heritage tramway from Sóller to Port de Sóller (p36).
Serveis Ferroviaris de Mallorca (SFM)
🌐 trensfm.com

Bus

Mallorca has an extensive island-wide bus network operated by CTM. The central hub is the Intermodal station at Plaça d'Espanya in Palma. Timetables and maps are available from the information office there, as well as on the CTM website.

Bus services within Palma are operated by **Empresa Municipal de Transports (EMT)**. They have dozens of routes that link the city centre and outer neighbourhoods; lines 4 and 25 are particularly useful for sightseeing and getting to the beach.

Empresa Municipal de Transports (EMT)

W emtpalma.cat

Metro

CTM also operates two metro lines on Mallorca, both of which depart from the Intermodal station at Plaça d'Espanya, in Palma. M1 runs north to the city's university, and M2 runs northeast to Marratxi. The service operates from 6:35am–9:35pm during weekdays with trains running every 20 minutes. Operating hours are reduced to 7am–2:30pm on Saturdays, while there is no service on Sundays.

Taxi

Taxis in Mallorca are white. **Palma Taxis** have a red stripe; in other municipalities the stripes are a different colour (check with your accomodation if you're unsure). Fares are moderate and there are plenty of taxis in circulation in Palma and in the main resorts, but fewer in rural areas. Supplements are charged for baggage and for fares to and from the airport and the ports.

Palma Taxis

W radiotaxiciutat.com

Driving

Driving is the only way to see some of the best sights on the island. If you plan on bringing a car into the country, you must carry a valid driving licence, plus insurance and car-registration documents at all times. You must also carry a warning triangle and fluorescent safety jacket in your car.

Spain has two types of motorway: *autopistas*, which are toll roads (prefixed with "AP"), and *autovías*, which are toll-free (prefixed with "A"). The Palma–Llucmajor, Palma–Sa Pobla and Palma–Manacor roads are the major highways. Other roads, though narrow and twisting, are mostly in good repair.

Roads and signage are generally good, although there is a shortage of hard shoulders. As a consequence, there are few opportunities to stop along the road and admire the scenery. Look out for cyclists and take great care when you are trying to reach some beaches or sights off the beaten track; the roads leading to them can be narrow, steep and winding, with few passing places.

All European and US driving licences are valid in Spain for tourists; visitors from North America are not required to have an International Driving Permit (IDP), but it is recommended.

Car Rental

Most big agencies, including **Avis**, **Hertz** and **Europcar**, are represented at Palma Airport. Drivers must be 21 or over, with a driver's licence and a credit card. Car seats for kids (compulsory for children under 135cm) cost extra. Note that you are not allowed to take hired cars from one island to another or from Mallorca to the mainland.

Avis

W avis.co.uk

Europcar

W europcar.co.uk

Hertz

W hertz.co.uk

Rules of the Road

Drive on the right and use the left lane only for passing other vehicles. You should be aware of the speed limits at all times. The fines for breaking the speed limits are high, just as they are for drink driving. The highest permitted blood alcohol level is 0.025 per cent.

Filling stations are common along main roads and in urban areas but thin on the ground when you are off the beaten track. Be aware that some petrol stations may close on Sundays. Many will have self-serve 24-hour pumps that require a chip-and-PIN credit card.

Rush hour only signficantly impacts Palma, but there may be tailbacks to and from tourist hotspots and the main beaches in the peak summer season.

Parking
Most car parks charge fees, and there are fines for non-payment. Paid car parking spaces along pavements are marked with a blue line. Generally, the parking fees apply from 9am to 1pm and from 5pm to 8pm on weekdays, and from 9am to 1pm on Saturdays. A yellow line painted along the pavement means that parking is prohibited.

Cycling
Mallorca is a very popular destination for biking, with a mix of country lanes and mountain roads that appeal to cyclists. The road to Sa Calobra is a particular highlight for serious bike enthusiasts, but there are numerous excellent routes to try all over the island. It is possible to cycle all year round, but conditions are most pleasant between October and May, when temperatures are not too hot. (Indeed, many professional cycling teams train here during the winter.)

Experienced cyclists (as well as those with no experience) can rent equipment at **Pro Cycle Hire** in Pollença. There are several suppliers in Palma and in many of the larger resorts, including **Nano Bicycles**, which also runs tours, and **Palma on Bike**. Palma also has a bike share system called **BiciPalma**, which allows people to pick up a bike from points around the city.

Mallorca Illes Balears *(p141)* has maps and GPX files for a network of 16 trails that connect the main towns and points of interest across the island.

These routes are well signed and have been graded by difficulty, making it possible to combine them into an itinerary according to your skill level and personal interests.

BiciPalma
W bicipalma.com
Nano Bicycles
W nanobicycles.com
Palma on Bike
W palmaonbike.com
Pro Cycle Hire
W procyclehire.com

Walking
Mallorca offers superb hiking routes, most notably the long-distance GR-221 *(p74)*. There are several mountain refuges offering accommodation along the route; the accommodation is basic, but simple meals are usually available (check in advance) and bedding can be rented if required. These refuges are maintained by the **Consell de Mallorca**. Advance booking for these is very strongly recommended.

The GR-222, another long-distance walking route that will eventually link Artà in the east with Lluc further west, is currently in development: some short sections, most around the north-east coast, are already open. Numerous shorter trails, many of which are ideal for families with young children, can be found in natural parks, such as the S'Albufera wetlands or the Parc Natural de Mondragó *(p122)*.

The Catalina Homar route is a wonderful 11-km- (6-mile-) long hike around Valldemossa. The start of the route is suitable for beginners, but only experienced hikers should carry on.

The Consell de Mallorca website has an excellent section dedicated to hikes across the island, with route maps available to download. It also has information on the GR-221. Mallorca Illes Balears *(p141)* also has information on the GR-221 and on family-friendly routes around the island.

Consell de Mallorca
W conselldemallorca.net

PRACTICAL INFORMATION

A little local know-how goes a long way in Mallorca. On these pages you can find all the essential advice and information you will need to make the most of your trip to this region.

AT A GLANCE

CURRENCY
Euro (EUR)

AVERAGE DAILY SPEND

SAVE
€60

SPEND
€165

SPLURGE
€300+

BOTTLED WATER
€1.50

COFFEE
€2.50

BEER
€6

DINNER FOR TWO
€60

ESSENTIAL PHRASES

Hello	Hola
Goodbye	Adiós
Please	Por favor
Thank you	Gracias
Do you speak English?	¿Habla inglés?
I don't understand...	No comprendo

ELECTRICITY SUPPLY

Power sockets are type F, fitting a two-prong, round-pin plug. Standard voltage is 230 volts.

Passports and Visas

For entry requirements, including visas, consult your nearest Spanish embassy or check the **Spanish Ministry of Foreign Affairs** website. Citizens of the UK, US, Canada, Australia and New Zealand do not need a visa for stays of up to three months, but in future must apply in advance for the European Travel Information and Authorization System (**ETIAS**); rollout has continually been postponed so check website for details. Visitors from other countries may also require an ETIAS, so check before travelling. EU nationals do not need a visa or an ETIAS.

ETIAS
W travel-europe.europa.eu/etias_en
Spanish Ministry of Foreign Affairs
W exteriores.gob.es

Government Advice

Now more than ever, it is important to consult both your and the Spanish government's advice before travelling. The UK Foreign, Commonwealth & Development Office (**FCDO**), the **US State Department**, the **Australian Department of Foreign Affairs and Trade** and the Spanish Ministry of Foreign Affairs offer the latest information on security, health and local regulations.

Australian Department of Foreign Affairs and Trade
W smartraveller.gov.au
FCDO
W gov.uk/foreign-travel-advice
US State Department
W travel.state.gov

Customs Information

You can find information on the laws relating to goods and currency taken in or out of Mallorca on the **Spanish Tax Office** website. Passengers can import different amounts of product from EU countries and non-EU country.

Spanish Tax Office
W agenciatributaria.es

Insurance

We recommend that you take out a comprehensive insurance policy covering theft, loss of belongings, medical care, cancellations and delays, and read the small print carefully. EU citizens are eligible for free emergency medical care in Spain provided they have a valid European Health Insurance Card (EHIC) or UK Global Health Insurance Card (**GHIC**).
GHIC
W ghic.org.uk

Money

All major credit cards are accepted in the larger hotels, restaurants and museums, but may not be accepted in smaller establishments. And while contactless payments are now common, it's a good idea to carry cash for smaller items. ATMs are readily available throughout the island. Spanish banks charge transaction fees, and your own bank may charge a fee for using non-branch machines.

Spain does not have a big tipping culture, but it is appreciated and it's common to round up the bill and usual to tip waiters 5–10 per cent.

Travellers with Specific Requirements

Mallorca is not especially well equipped for visitors with specific requirements, although things are improving. The uneven streets of Palma's historic quarter are difficult to negotiate with a wheelchair, and some sights remain wholly or partially inaccessible to those with limited mobility. However, most newer attractions, hotels and restaurants are wheelchair-accessible, as is all public transport.

Spain's **COCEMFE** (Confederación Española de Personas con Discapacidad Física y Orgánica) provides useful information, while companies such as **Disabled Accessible Travel** and **Accessible Spain Travel** offer specialist tours for those with reduced mobility, sight and hearing.

The official tourist website, **Mallorca Illes Balears**, has been designed to help those with impaired sight and hearing: visit the "Web Accessibility" section for more information.
Accessible Spain Travel
W accessiblespaintravel.com
COCEMFE
W cocemfe.es
Disabled Accessible Travel
W disabledaccessibletravel.com
Mallorca Illes Balears
W mallorca.es

Languages

The local language is Mallorquí, a dialect of Catalan, but Castilian (Spanish) is also spoken everywhere. Signs are usually in Catalan. It is perfectly acceptable to speak Castilian but any efforts to speak Mallorquí, even a simple *bon dia* (good day) is usually warmly received. English is widely spoken in cities and tourist spots, but not always in rural areas.

Opening Hours

Shops in Mallorca are usually open Monday to Saturday from 9:30am until 8 or 9pm, and close for lunch around 1:30 or 2pm to 4:30 or 5pm. In the larger towns and resorts, big chains and department stores open from 10am to 9pm and do not close for lunch. They are often open on Sundays. Shops in the larger resorts may open only at weekends or even close during the winter.

Banks are open 9:30am to 2pm, and some also open on Thursday afternoons from 4 to 7pm, though a few operate a reduced timetable in summer. Churches open 8am to 1pm and from 6 to 8pm; some are open on Sunday mornings but prefer not to admit tourists.

Situations can change quickly and unexpectedly. Always check before visiting attractions and hospitality venues for up-to-date opening hours and booking requirements.

Personal Security

Mallorca is a relatively safe place to visit, but petty crime does take place. Pickpockets work known tourist areas, beaches and busy streets. Use your common sense and be alert to your surroundings, and you should enjoy a stress-free trip.

If you do have anything stolen, report the crime within 24 hours to the nearest police station (*comissaria*) where contact is generally with the **Policía Local** (local police). Take ID with you and make sure to get a copy of the crime report if you plan to make an insurance claim. Contact your embassy if your passport is stolen, or in the event of a serious crime.

As a rule, Spaniards are accepting of all people, regardless of their race, gender or sexuality. Homosexuality was legalized in Spain in 1979 and in 2007, the government recognized same-sex marriage and adoption rights for same-sex couples. Palma is where many of the best LGBTQ+ venues are found, along with the **Ella International Lesbian Festival**. If you do feel unsafe while in Mallorca, head for the nearest police station.

Ella International Lesbian Festival
w ellafestival.com
Policía Local
c 092 (emergency)
c 971 225500

Health

Spain has a world-class healthcare system. Emergency medical care in Spain is free for all UK and EU citizens. If you have an EHIC or GHIC (*p141*), be sure to present this as soon as possible. You may have to pay after treatment and reclaim the money later. For other visitors, payment of medical expenses is the patient's responsibility. It is therefore important to arrange comprehensive insurance before travelling.

If you do fall ill, Palma has two main public hospitals: Hospital de Sant Joan de Déu and Hospital Universitario Son Espases. Otherwise, pharmacies (*farmacias*) are a good source of advice for minor complaints, identifiable by a green or red cross. When closed, they are required to post a list of pharmacies on duty (*farmàcies de guàrdia*), also available through the **COFIB** website.

COFIB
w cofib.es

AT A GLANCE

EMERGENCY NUMBERS

GENERAL EMERGENCY	FIRE SERVICE
112	**18**

POLICE	MEDICAL EMERGENCY
17	**15**

TIME ZONE
CET/CEST: Central European Summer time runs from the last Sunday in March to the last Sunday in October.

TAP WATER
Unless stated otherwise, tap water in Mallorca is safe to drink.

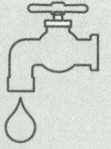

WEBSITES AND APPS

Mallorca Tourist Information
The official website for tourist information on Mallorca (*Mallorca.es*).
Visit Palma
The city's website for tourists (*visitpalma.com*).
Balear Coast
This website and app provide real-time beach information (*balearcoast.es*).
MobiPalma
The official app for transport in Palma with live updates on traffic and parking.

Smoking, Alcohol and Drugs

Smoking is banned in enclosed public spaces and is a fineable offence, though you can still smoke on the terraces of bars and restaurants. Spain has a relaxed attitude towards alcohol consumption, but it is frowned upon to be openly drunk and drinking in public is not permitted in certain areas.

Recreational drugs are illegal, and possession of even a very small quantity can lead to an extremely hefty fine or a custodial sentence.

Responsible Travel

Climate change is having an increasing impact on Mallorca through droughts and forest fires. In response, the island has pioneered sustainable solutions such as the Sustainable Tourism Tax, introduced in 2016, and the 2021 ban on single-use plastics.

Do your bit by limiting water usage, reusing items such as towels and carrying a reusable water bottle, which can be refilled at public drinking fountains found across the island.

Additionally, some locals have become frustrated with tourists, citing poor behaviour, drunkenness and the negative impact of tourism. As such, enjoy the island with respect for the traditions and locals who live here, and help them in preserving the island for future generations to enjoy.

ID

By law you must carry identification with you at all times in Spain. A photocopy of your passport should suffice, but you may be asked to report to a police station with the original document.

Local Customs

Regional pride is strong throughout Spain. Be wary of referring to Catalans, Galicians and Basques as "Spanish", as this can sometimes cause offence. A Spanish tradition is the siesta, which sees some places close between 1pm and 5pm. This is not always observed by large stores or in very touristy areas.

Mobile Phones and Wi-Fi

Mobile-phone coverage in Mallorca is good. Visitors on EU tariffs can use their devices without being affected by data roaming charges. Visitors from other countries should check their contracts or consider picking up a Spanish SIM card.

Free Wi-Fi is reasonably common, particularly in libraries, large public spaces, restaurants and bars. Many cafés, hotels and restaurants also offer free Wi-Fi to patrons.

Postal Services

Correos is Spain's postal service. Letters take about three to five days to arrive in other EU countries, and five to seven days to arrive in North America. There are post offices in larger towns and resorts while yellow letterboxes are found across the island.
Correos
🅆 correos.es

Taxes and Refunds

IVA in the Balearic Islands is normally 21 per cent, but with lower rates for certain goods and services. Under certain conditions, non-EU citizens can claim a rebate of these taxes. Present a form and your receipts to a customs officer at your point of departure.

Tours

All manner of trips and tours are available in Mallorca and local tourist offices can offer information on the options available in the area. If you are looking for thrills, operators including **Mallorca Adventure Sports** and **Experience Mallorca** offer a range of outdoor and adventure activities. There are also plenty of more sedate options, such as a tour of the best vineyards with **Mallorca Wine Tours**.
Experience Mallorca
🅆 experience-mallorca.com
Mallorca Adventure Sports
🅆 mallorcaadventuresports.com
Mallorca Wine Tours
🅆 mallorcawinetours.com

PLACES TO STAY

From family-friendly chains to hilltop monasteries, luxury boutiques to urban hostels, Mallorca has accommodation in abundance. Sun-seekers can lap up rays at a beachfront stay while the more adventurous can explore the rural interior, with its traditional villages.

Prices and crowds rise in the summer (July–August) but ease off in spring and autumn. In larger towns, hotels may open year-round but some resorts close seasonally. A tourist tax is payable with a sliding scale depending on accommodation (under-16s are exempt).

PRICE CATEGORIES

For a standard double room per night (with breakfast if included), taxes and extra charges.

€ under €100
€€ $100–€250
€€€ over €250

Palma

Nakar Hotel

🗺 K3 🏠 Av. de Jaume III, 21 🌐 nakarhotel.com · €€

This sharp contemporary hotel is located on one of Palma's busiest shopping arteries. Step inside, however, and it's all calm and quiet, from its serene subterranean spa to its rooftop pool with panoramic views. Dining in is a treat: Nakar's restaurant Cuit is run by one of Mallorca's top chefs, Miquel Calent.

Urban Hostel Palma

🗺 C4 🏠 Plaça de la Verge del Miracle, 4 🌐 urban hostelpalma.com · €

Want to be in Palma's happening Santa Catalina district without breaking the bank? Then Urban Hostel is the place for you. These hip lodgings, overlooking a pretty plaza, are ideally located, just minutes from the bars, clubs and restaurants of the area. A guest dining room and well-appointed kitchen are ideal for those who want to whip up a meal at any hour.

Innside Bosque

🗺 C4 🏠 C/Camilo José Cela, 5 🌐 melia.com · €€

Friendly staff are what set this chic hotel, part of the Meliá group, apart. There's no need too great, from recommending a day trip, directions to the city's sights or booking a treatment at the hotel's luxurious spa. At its centre you'll find a shimmering pool where bookable Bali beds and a poolside bar give a laid-back, beach-club vibe.

Can Bordoy

🗺 L4 🏠 C/del Forn de la Glòria, 14 🌐 canbordoy.com · €€€

Tucked away deep in the lanes of Palma's Old Town, this 16th-century mansion has been sumptuously restyled with a mix of historic glamour and modern elegance (think Gothic pillars, Baroque mirrors and modern furnishings). Rooms are reassuringly cosy (with firmness-adjustable beds), while a spa and two outdoor pools provide plenty of space to relax in.

El Llorenç Parc de la Mar

🗺 P6 🏠 Plaça de Llorenç Villalonga, 4 🌐 elllorenc.com · €€€

Mediterranean-Swedish design may not be the obvious combination, but it works perfectly at this jazzy hotel. Designer Magnus Ehrland has created a warm environment by combining Moorish motifs, colourful artworks and retro touches that hark back to the 1920s. Better yet, the Michelin-starred restaurant on site is one of Palma's best eateries.

Brick Palma

🗺 P4 🏠 C/del Forn d'en Vila, 3 (53) 🌐 staybrich.es · €€

Somewhere between a hotel and a hostel, and set in a mid-19th century former pottery factory, this central Palma spot has an industrial hipster vibe that attracts a younger crowd. Its on-site bar is always buzzing with guests and locals, making it the perfect place to get to know your new neighbours.

Southwest Coast
. . . .

Zel Mallorca
⑨ B4 ⬛C/Duc Estremera, 16, Calvià 🌐 melia.com · €€€

This beachfront hotel is a collaboration between Mallorcan chain Meliá and the island's most iconic sportsman, Rafa Nadal. Don't worry, there's no tennis-themed decor, just breezy Mediterranean styling, with plenty of natural light. The best bit? Palmanova's trio of beautiful beaches are right outside.

The Donna Portals
⑨ C4 ⬛C/Falconer, 19, Portals Nous 🌐 thedonna portals.com · €€€

This bang-on-the-beach hotel, by Dutch design doyen Marcel Wanders, is opulence dialled up to 11. It has all the luxe touches you'd expect (a bells-and-whistles spa, swish steak-and-lobster restaurant, and champagne bar) and some you would never expect, such as "themed suites" designed around retro gaming, a sauna or stargazing (including your own telescope).

Castell Son Claret
⑨ B4 ⬛Carretera hm 1.7 Calvià 🌐 castellsonclaret. com · €€€

Ever wanted to feel like royalty? Then book a stay at arguably Mallorca's most luxurious hotel, a former castle complete with crenellated towers. Explore your kingdom of over 120 hectares (300 acres) or nab a pool suite to relax in a private pool and garden. Finish the day with a meal fit for a monarch at the Michelin-starred Sa Castra.

Hostel Sóller
⑨ C2 ⬛C/de Santa Teresa, 27, Sóller 🌐 hostel soller.com · €€€

Choose a private room or a dorm at this beautiful Modernist building, in the heart of historic Sóller. The communal areas, filled with books, bean-bags and a cosy fireplace, are the perfect place to relax or make friends, before checking out the hostel's suggested hiking and biking routes.

Fergus Club Mallorca Waterpark
⑨ B4 ⬛Avda. Las Palmeras, 12, Magaluf 🌐 fergushotels.com · €€

Unleash your inner child at this all-inclusive hotel's incredible waterpark, the biggest such park in the Balearics. Kids and adults alike will love making a splash with some serious waterslide action. And when you need a break, drop the little ones at the kids' club so you can relax with a holiday read on the in-pool loungers.

Hospes Maricel
⑨ C4 ⬛Ctra. Andratx, 11, Palma 🌐 hospes.com/ maricel-spa · €€€

Follow in the footsteps of Hollywood icons Errol Flynn and Montgomery Clift with a stay at the south coast's most iconic hotel. Hospes blends elegant Art Nouveau features with modern stone and wood designs to striking effect. And best of all, Hospes holds the title of "The Best Breakfast in the World", with an extravagent tasting menu that ranges from *Huevo de Onsen* (eggs in potato foam) to prickly pear sorbet with Champagne.

Universal Hotel Aquamarin
⑨ A4 ⬛C/Cala es Conills, 4, Sant Elm 🌐 universal hotelaquamarin.com · €€

Spring for a water-facing room at this resort and you'll have front-row seats to the most spectacular view in Mallorca: sunset over Dragonera Island. Spend the rest of your time indulging at the sea-view spa or relaxing on the two sandy beaches located just steps away from the hotel.

Hotel Esplendido
⑨ C2 ⬛Passeig es Traves, 5, Port de Sóller 🌐 esplen didohotel.com · €€€

Stroll down Port Sóller's promenade and you can't miss the imposing stone façade of this hotel. A thorough face-lift hasn't diminished the vintage vibe that pervades the Esplendido. Inside you'll find modern amenities (thermal pool, luxury spa and wellnes studio) complemented by period features such as vinyl records, retro furniture and that original façade.

North Coast

Hotel Can Mostatxins

9 F2 **🏠** C/del Lledoner, 15, Alcúdia **W** hotelcan mostatxins.com · €€

Painstakingly converted from a pair of pretty 15th-century townhouses, this is one of Alcúdia's most-loved boutique hotels. Its eight rooms give it an air of exclusivity while the pair of tower suites, with private access via a glass walkway, feel like something straight out of a fairy tale.

Son Brull

9 E2 **🏠** Crta. Palma–Pollença PM 220, ĥm 50 **W** sonbrull.com · €€€

With its unique rustic-luxe-meets-Scandi-chic design, this elegantly restored 18th-century monastery is certainly a magical place to stay. But it's the back-to-nature setting that steals the show. The monastery is surrounded by olive, scented lavender and citrus trees, and vast farmlands, which produce the food used in the hotel's lovely restaurant.

Es Blau des Nord

9 G3 **🏠** C/des Pla de Mar, Urbanització s'Estanyol **W** esblaudesnord.com · €€

If the hubbub of urban areas is too noisy for you, this coastal complex on the quieter eastern end of Alcúdia's bay offers a serene and secluded stay. The minimalist rooms are flooded with light and many have either a sea or garden view. Best of all, a pristine beach is on your doorstep with a world of watersports.

Mar Calma Hotel

9 E1 **🏠** C/de Formentor, 17 **W** marcalmahotel.com · €

With its buzzy cocktail bar, walk-in rainfall showers and rooftop jacuzzi with sea views, this modestly priced spot in Port de Pollença might just be the best-value stay in town. It's tempting to stay in and soak up the views from the hotel, but step outside and you're just a flip-flop shuffle from the beach or the historic sites of Pollença.

Zafiro Palace Alcudia

9 F2 **🏠** C/del Camí Reial al Moll, 2, Alcúdia **W** zafiro hotels.com · €€€

This is one of Mallorca's best family-friendly, five-star hotels, with a little something for everyone. A bubble-dome pool, mini-waterpark and giant pirate ship provide endless amounts of fun for little holidaymakers. Meanwhile, adults can sip cocktails at the swim-up bar, kick back on loungers in the kid-free zone or luxuriate in the spa.

Southeast Coast

Hostal Playa

9 E6 **🏠** C/Major 25, Colònia de Sant Jordi **W** restaurant eplaya.com · €

This family-run spot is unashamedly traditional and offers a glimpse into what Mallorca was like, before overtourism set in. Inside the typical Mallorcan townhouse you'll find high ceilings, wooden beams and beautifully crafted paintings, all by local artists. Outside the house is an on-site restaurant and a quiet beach that you could well have all to yourself.

Hotel Apartaments Playa Mondragó

9 F6 **🏠** Cala Mondragó, s/n **W** playamondrago. com · €€

Locations don't come more special than this. These modern lodgings are tucked away in the protected Mondragó Natural Park and are just steps from one of the island's best beaches, Cala Mondragó. There may be no better feeling than waking up to a view of the shimmering sea, just outside your window.

Can Ferrereta

9 F6 **🏠** C/Can Ferrereta, 12, Santanyí **W** hotelcan ferrereta.com · €€€

If you want to know where travel tastemakers flock, look no further than this thoroughly modern hotel, set in an immaculately restyled 17th-century townhouse. Impeccable service, luxury amenities and a curated selection of art and photography combine to make this one of the island's best boltholes. Then there's the Santanyí setting that's within reach of many selfie-worthy coves and beaches.

Hotel Predi Son Jaumell

🏨 H3 🏠 Ctra. Cala Mesquida, hm 1 🖥 hotel sonjaumell.com · €€

This 14th-century estate inhabits a blissful slice of bucolic Mallorca. Step out of the arty and minimalist interior and you'll find yourself transported into a verdant world of fragrant Mediterranean gardens, orchards, farmland, vineyards and even a Bronze Age cave.

Eques Petit Resort

🏨 F6 🏠 Avda. de Calonge, 9, Santanyí 🖥 equespetit resort.com · €€

Back in the 1960s, the formerly named Hotel Club Hipico was a pioneering tourism hotel. After a thorough renovation, and a new name, it's set to be a pioneer in accessible tourism. The hotel has barrier-free access, with several wheelchair-accessible bathrooms, and a zero-entry pool that all can enjoy.

Sant Salvador Hostatgeria

🏨 F5 🏠 Puig San Salvador, s/n 🖥 cancalcohotels. com/en/sant-salvador-hostatgeria · €

This carefully restored ancient monastery may be a little basic, but it's the spectacular setting atop a mountain that attracts guests. There are few better ways to start the day than stepping outside with a morning coffee to take in the view below. Just don't forget to explore the historic monastery itself; some parts have been little changed since 1348.

Central Plain

Es Figueral Nou Hotel

🏨 E4 🏠 C/de Montuiri a Sant Joan, hm 7, Montuïri 🖥 esfigueralnou.es · €€€

The rolling patchwork of fields that surrounds this rural hideaway makes it one of the more beautiful settings in Mallorca. The hotel is easy on the eye, too, its 18th-century stone arches and vaulted ceilings blending artfully with smart contemporary styling. A kids-free environment guarantees tranquillity, while a bijou spa and gorgeous pool are the cherries on top.

Hotel Rural S'Olivaret

🏨 D3 🏠 C/Alaró-Orient, hm 3 🖥 solivaret.com · €€

Escape from the urban sprawl and get back to nature at this vast estate. The sensitively restored 14th-century manor looks out over a luminescent turquoise pool and is surrounded by lush greenery, thick woodlands and landscaped terraces. Hulking over it all is the pine-carpeted escarpment of Puig de s'Alcadena, perfect for adventurous hikes.

Ten Mallorca

🏨 E3 🏠 C/de Son Riera, 10 🖥 tenmallorca.com· €€

Tucked down a narrow lane in the heart of Sineu, this converted priory is anything but ordinary. Eye-catching mono images of Hollywood icons plaster the walls, colourful furniture is everywhere and all of the nine rooms are uniquely designed, with quirky wallpaper and fun additions like pink flamingoes. It's the perfect place for a different escape.

Son Sant Andreu Agroturismo

🏨 F4 🏠 Ctra. Petra a Felanitx, hm 2 🖥 sonsant andreu.com · €€

Fancy yourself as a budding chef? Then book a stay at this venerable 17th-century estate, which bucks the norm in offering the traditional charm of a Mallorcan finca while giving guests the freedom to cook across three shared kitchens and a barbecue area. Where better to make use of the island's locally grown bounty?

Hostatgeria del Santuari de Cura

🏨 E4 🏠 Puig de Randa 🖥 santuaridecura.com · €

This former monastery has a storied history dating back several centuries – the venerated Catalan mystic and poet, Roman Llull, mentioned it in his 1311 book *Vida Coetania*. If its history doesn't tempt you then maybe the views will: the hotel sits on the highest point in the central plains, the sacred mountain of Puig de Randa, and has breathtaking island-wide panoramas to enjoy.

INDEX

PHRASE BOOK

In an Emergency

Help!	Auxili!	ow-gzee-lee
Stop!	Pareu!	pah-reh-oo
Call a doctor!	Telefoneu un metge!	teh-leh-fon-eh-oo oon meh-djuh
Call an ambulance!	Telefoneu una ambulància!	teh-leh-fon-eh-oo oo-nah ahm-boo-lahn-see-ah
Call the police!	Telefoneu la policia	teh-leh-fon-eh-oo lah poh-lee see-ah
Call the fire brigade!	Telefoneu els bombers!	teh-leh-fon-eh-oo uhlz boom-behs
Where is the nearest telephone?	On és el teléfon més proper?	on-ehs uhl tuh-leh fon mehs proo-peh
Where is the nearest hospital?	On és l'hospital més proper?	on-ehs looss-pee-tahl mehs proo-peh

Communication Essentials

Yes	Sí	see
No	No	noh
Please	Per favor	pair fa-vor
Thank you	Gràcies	grah-see-uhs
Excuse me	Perdona	puhr-thoh-na
Hello	Hola	oh-lah
Goodbye	Adéu	ah-they-oo
Good night	Bona nit	bo-nah neet
Morning	El matí	uhl muh-tee
Afternoon	La tarda	lah tahr-thuh
Evening	El vespre	uhl vehs-pruh
Yesterday	Ahir	ah-ee
Today	Avui	uh-voo-ee
Tomorrow	Demà	duh-mah
Here	Aquí	uh-kee
There	Allà	uh-lyah
What?	Qué?	keh
When?	Quan?	Kwahn
Why?	Per qué?	puhr keh
Where?	On?	ohn

Useful Phrases

How are you?	Com està?	kom uhs-tah
Very well, thank you.	Molt bé, gràcies.	mol beh grah-see-uhs
Pleased to meet you.	Molt de gust.	mol duh goost
See you soon.	Fins aviat.	feenz uhv-yat
That's fine.	Està bé.	uhs-tah beh
Where is/are … ?	On és/són … ?	ohn ehs/sohn
How far is it to… ?	Quants metres/ kilòmetres hi ha d'aquí a … ?	kwahnz meh-truhs/kee-loh-muh-truhs yah dah-kee uh
Which way to … ?	Per on es va a … ?	puhr on uhs bah ah
Do you speak English?	Parla anglés?	par-luh an-glehs
I don't understand.	No l'entenc.	noh luhn-teng
Could you speak more slowly, please?	Pot parlar més a poc a poc, si us plau?	pot par-lah mehs pok uh pok sees plah-oo
I'm sorry.	Ho sento.	oo sehn-too

Useful Words

big	gran	gran
small	petit	puh-teet
hot	calent	kah-len
cold	fred	fred
good	bo	boh
bad	dolent	doo-len
enough	bastant	bahs-tan
well	bé	beh
open	obert	oo-behr
closed	tancat	tan-kat
left	esquerra	uhs-kehr-ruh
right	dreta	dreh-tuh
straight on	recte	rehk-tuh
near	a prop	uh prop
far	lluny	lyoonyuh
up/over	a dalt	uh dahl
down/under	a baix	uh bah-eeshh
early	aviat	uhv-yat
late	tard	tahrt
entrance	entrada	uhn-trah-thuh
exit	sortida	soor-tee-thuh
toilet	lavabos/ serveis	luh-vah-boos sehr-beh-ees
more	més	mess
less	menys	menyees

Shopping

How much does this cost?	Quant costa això?	kwahn kost ehs-shoh
I would like …	M'agradaria …	muh-grah-thuh-ree-ah
Do you have?	Tenen?	tehn-un
I'm just looking, thank you.	Només estic mirant, gràcies.	noo -mess ehs-teek mee-rahn grah-see-uhs
Do you take credit cards?	Accepten targes de crédit?	ak-sehp-tuhn tahr-zhuhs duh kreh-deet
What time do you open?	A quina hora obren?	ah keen-uh oh-ruh oh-bruhn
What time do you close?	A quina hora tanquen?	ah keen-uh oh ruh tan-kuhn
This one.	Aquest.	ah-ket
That one.	Aquell.	ah-kehl
expensive	car	kahr
cheap	bé de preu/ barat	beh thuh preh-oo/bah-rat
size (clothes)	talla/mida	tah-lyah/ mee-thuh
size (shoes)	número	noo-mehr-oo
white	blanc	blang
black	negre	neh-gruh
red	vermell	vuhr-mel
yellow	groc	grok
green	verd	behrt
blue	blau	blah-oo
antiques shop	antiquari/ botiga d'antiguitats	an-tee-kwah-ree/ boo-tee-gah/dan-tee-ghee-tats
bakery	el forn	uhl forn
bank	el banc	uhl bang
bookshop	la llibreria	lah lyee-bruh-ree-ah

butcher's	la carnisseria	lah kahr-nee-suh-**ree**-uh
fishmonger's	la peixateria	lah peh-shuh-tuh-**ree**-uh
greengrocer's	la fruiteria	lah froo-ee-tuh-**ree**-uh
grocer's	la botiga de queviures	lah boo-**tee**-guh duh keh-vee-**oo**-ruhs
hairdresser's	la perruqueria	lah peh-roo-kuh-**ree**-uh
market	el mercat	uhl muhr-**kat**
newsagent's	el quiosc de premsa	uhl kee-**ohsk** duh **prem**-suh
pastry shop	la pastisseria	lah pahs-tee-suh-**ree**-uh
pharmacy	la farmàcia	lah fuhr-**mah**-see-ah
post office	l'oficina de correus	loo-fee-**see**-nuh duh koo-**reh**-oos
shoe shop	la sabateria	lah sah-bah-tuh-**ree**-uh
supermarket	el supermercat	uhl soo-puhr-muhr-**kat**
tobacconist's	l'estanc	luhs-**tang**
travel agency	l'agència de viatges	la-**jen**-see-uh duh vee-**ad**-juhs

Sightseeing

art gallery	la galeria d' art	lah gah-luh **ree**-yuh **dart**
cathedral	la catedral	lah kuh-tuh-**thrahl**
church	l'església/ la basílica	luhz-**gleh**-zee-uh/ lah buh-**zee**-lee-kuh
garden	el jardí	uhl zhahr-**dee**
library	la biblioteca	lah bee-blee-oo-**teh**-kuh
museum	el museu	uhl moo-**seh**-oo
tourist infor-mation office	l'oficina de turisme	loo-fee-**see**-nuh thuh too-**reez**-muh
town hall	l'ajuntament	luh-djoon-tuh-**men**
closed for holiday	tancat per vacances	tan-**kat** puhr bah-**kan**-suhs
bus station	l'estació d'autobusos	luhs-tah-see-**oh** dow-toh-**boo**-zoos
railway station	l'estació de tren	luhs-tah-see-**oh** thuh **tren**

Staying in a Hotel

Do you have a vacant room?	Tenen una habitació lliure?	**teh**-nuhn oo-nuh ah-bee-tuh-see-**oh** **lyuh**-ruh
double room with a double bed	habitació doble amb llit de matrimoni	ah-bee-tuh-see-**oh** **doh**-bluh am **lyeet** duh mah-tree-**moh**-nee
twin room	habitació amb dos llits/ amb llits individuals	ah-bee-tuh-see-**oh** am dohs **lyeets**/ am **lyeets** in-thee-vee-thoo-**ahls**

single room	habitació individual	ah-bee-tuh-see-**oh** een-dee-vee-thoo-**ahl**
room with a bath	habitació amb bany	ah-bee-tuh-see-**oh** am **bahn**-yuh
shower	dutxa	**doo**-chuh
porter	el grum	uhl **groom**
key	la clau	lah **klah**-oo
I have a reservation.	Tinc una habitació reservada	**ting** oo-nuh ah-bee-tuh-see-**oh** reh-sehr-**vah**-thah

Eating Out

Have you got a table for …	Tenen taula per … ?	**teh**-nuhn **tow**-luh puhr
I would like to reserve a table.	Voldria reservar una taula.	vool-**dree**-uh reh-sehr-**vahr** oo-nuh **tow**-luh
The bill, please.	El compte, si us plau.	uhl **kohm**-tuh sees **plah**-oo
I am a vegetarian.	Sóc vegetarià/ vegetariana.	**sok** buh-zhuh-tuh-ree-**ah** buh-zhuh-tuh-ree-**ah**-nah
waitress	cambrera	kam-**breh**-ruh
waiter	cambrer	kam-**breh**
menu	la carta	lah **kahr**-tuh
fixed-price menu	menú del dia	muh-**noo** thuhl **dee**-uh
wine list	la carta de vins	lah **kahr**-tuh thuh **veens**
glass of water	un got d'aigua	oon got dah-ee-gwah
glass of wine	una copa de vi	oo-nuh ko-pah thuh **vee**
bottle	una ampolla	oo-nuh am-**pol**-yuh
knife	un ganivet	oon gun-ee-**veht**
fork	una forquilla	oo-nuh foor-**keel**-yuh
spoon	una cullera	oo-nuh kool-**yeh**-ruh
breakfast	l'esmorzar	les-moor-**sah**
lunch	el dinar	uhl dee-**nah**
dinner	el sopar	uhl soo-**pah**
main course	el primer plat	uhl pree-**meh plat**
starters	els entrants	uhlz ehn-**tranz**
dish of the day	el plat del dia	uhl **plat** duhl **dee**-uh
coffee	el café	uhl kah-**feh**
rare	poc fet	**pok fet**
medium	al punt	ahl **poon**
well done	molt fet	**mol fet**

Menu Decoder

l'aigua mineral	**lah**-ee-gwuh mee-nuh-**rahl**	mineral water
sense gas/ amb gas	sen-zuh gas/ am gas	still/ sparkling
al forn	ahl **forn**	baked
l'all	**lahl**yuh	garlic
l'arròs	lahr-**roz**	rice

les botifarres	lahs **boo**-tee-fah-rahs	sausages
la carn	lah **karn**	meat
la ceba	lah **seh**-buh	onion
la cervesa	lah-sehr-**ve**-sah	beer
l'embotit	lum-boo-**teet**	cold meat
el filet	uhl fee-**let**	sirloin
el formatge	uhl for-**mah**-djuh	cheese
fregit	freh-**zheet**	fried
la fruita	lah froo-ee-tah	fruit
els fruits secs	uhlz froo-eets seks	nuts
les gambes	lahs **gam**-bus	prawns
el gelat	uhl djuh-**lat**	ice cream
la llagosta	lah lyah-**gos**-tah	lobster
la llet	lah **lyet**	milk
la llimona	lah lyee-**moh**-nah	lemon
la llimonada	lah lyee-moh-**nah**-thuh	lemonade
la mantega	lah mahn-**teh**-gah	butter
el marisc	uhl muh-**reesk**	seafood
la menestra	lah muh-**nehs**-truh	vegetable stew
l'oli	**loll**-ee	oil
les olives	luhs oo-**lee**-vuhs	olives
l'ou	**loh**-oo	egg
el pa	uhl **pah**	bread
el pastís	uhl pahs-**tees**	pie/cake
les patates	lahs pah-**tah**-tuhs	potatoes
el pebre	uhl **peh**-bruh	pepper
el peix	uhl **pehsh**	fish
el pernil	uhl puhr-**neel**	cured ham
salat serrà	suh-**lat** sehr-**rah**	
el plàtan	uhl **plah**-tun	banana
el pollastre	uhl poo-**lyah**-struh	chicken
la poma	la **poh**-mah	apple
el porc	uhl **pohr**	pork
els postres	lahs **pohs**-truhs	dessert
rostit	rohs-**teet**	roast
la sal	lah **sahl**	salt
la salsa	lah **sahl**-suh	sauce
les salsitxes	lahs sahl-**see**-chuhs	sausages
sec	**sehk**	dry
la sopa	lah **soh**-puh	soup
el sucre	uhl-**soo**-kruh	sugar
la taronja	lah tuh-**rohn**-djuh	orange
el te	uhl **teh**	tea
les torrades	lahs too-**rah**-thuhs	toast
la vedella	lah veh-**theh**-lyuh	beef
el vi blanc	uhl **bee blang**	white wine
el vi negre	uhl **bee neh**-gruh	red wine
el vi rosat	uhl **bee** roo-**zaht**	rosé wine
el vinagre	uhl bee-**nah**-gruh	vinegar
el xai/el be	uhl **shahee**/ uhl **beh**	lamb
la xocolata	lah shoo-koo-**lah**-tuh	chocolate
el xoriç	uhl shoo-**rees**	red sausage

Numbers

0	zero	**seh**-roo
1	un (masc)	oon
	una (fem)	**oon**-uh
2	dos (masc)	**dohs**
	dues (fem)	**doo**-uhs
3	tres	**trehs**
4	quatre	**kwa**-truh
5	cinc	**seeng**
6	sis	**sees**
7	set	**set**
8	vuit	**voo**-eet
9	nou	**noh**-oo
10	deu	**deh**-oo
11	onze	**on**-zuh
12	dotze	**doh**-dzuh
13	tretze	**treh**-dzuh
14	catorze	kah-**tohr**-dzuh
15	quinze	**keen**-zuh
16	setze	**set**-zuh
17	disset	dee-**set**
18	divuit	dee-voo-**eet**
19	dinou	dee-**noh**-oo
20	vint	**been**
21	vint-i-un	been-tee-**oon**
22	vint-i-dos	been-tee-**dohs**
30	trenta	**tren**-tah
31	trenta-un	tren-**tah** oon
40	quaranta	kwuh-**ran**-tuh
50	cinquanta	seen-**kwahn**-tah
60	seixanta	seh-ee-**shan**-tah
70	setanta	seh-**tan**-tah
80	vuitanta	voo-ee-**tan**-tah
90	noranta	noh-**ran**-tah
100	cent	**sen**
101	cent un	**sent** oon
102	cent dos	**sen dohs**
200	dos-cents (masc)	dohs-**sens**
	dues-centes (masc)	**doo**-uhs sen-**tuhs**
300	tres-cents	trehs-**senz**
400	quatre-cents	kwah-truh-**senz**
500	cinc-cents	seeng-**senz**
600	sis-cents	sees-**senz**
700	set-cents	set-**senz**
800	vuit-cents	voo-eet-**senz**
900	nou-cents	noh-oo-**cenz**
1,000	mil	**meel**
1,001	mil un	**meel** oon

Time

one minute	un minut	oon mee-**noot**
one hour	una hora	oo-nuh oh-ruh
half an hour	mitja hora	**mee**-juh oh-ruh
Monday	dilluns	dee-**lyoonz**
Tuesday	dimarts	dee-**marts**
Wednesday	dimecres	dee-**meh**-kruhs
Thursday	dijous	dee-**zhoh**-oos
Friday	divendres	dee-**ven**-druhs
Saturday	dissabte	dee-**sab**-tuh
Sunday	diumenge	dee-oo-**men**-juh

ACKNOWLEDGMENTS

This edition updated by

Contributor Leon Beckenham

Senior Editor Alison McGill

Senior Designers Laura O'Brien, Vinita Venugopal

Project Editor Charlie Baker

Editor Ilina Choudhary

Project Art Editor Bineet Kaur

Proofreader Samantha Cook

Indexer Helen Peters

Picture Research Deputy Manager Virien Chopra

Senior Picture Researcher Nishwan Rasool

Assistant Picture Research Administrator Manpreet Kaur

Publishing Assistant Simona Velikova

Jacket Designers Laura O'Brien, Bineet Kaur

Senior Cartographers Subhashree Bharati, James Macdonald

Cartography Manager Suresh Kumar

DTP Designer Rohit Rojal

Pre-production Manager Balwant Singh

Image Retouching-Production Manager Pankaj Sharma

Senior Production Controller Samantha Cross

Managing Editors Beverly Smart, Hollie Teague

Managing Art Editors Gemma Doyle, Priyanka Thakur

Art Director Maxine Pedliham

Publishing Director Georgina Dee

DK would like to thank the following for their contribution to the previous editions: Ian Aitken, Mary-Ann Gallagher, Jeffrey Kennedy, Phil Lee, Clare Peel, Helen Peters, Suzanne Porter, Colin Sinclair.

The publisher would like to thank the following for their kind permission to reproduce their photographs:

Key: a-above; b-below/bottom; c-centre; f-far; l-left; r-right; t-top

Alamy Stock Photo: Agencja Fotograficzna Caro / Stefanie Preuss 45t, Album 9br, 13clb, 59, 104bl, 129t, Peter Alvey 64t, Associated Press / Tomàs Moyà 10bl, Tolo Balaguer 60b, 67t, 85, 106, Bildagentur-online 39t, 47b, blickwinkel / D. Berg 73, Hans Blossey 53b, CFimages 81b, Loetscher Chlaus 51t, Classic Image 8, Emily Wilson / DanitaDelimont 52, directphoto.bz 20cla, Greg Balfour Evans 86–87b, 98, F1online digitale Bildagentur GmbH / Siepmann 131tl, Peter Forsberg 16crb, FPW 13cl, freeartist 21br, John Freeman 58t, GL Archive 10tl, 10br, Maisant Ludovic / Hemis.fr 60t, Sierpinski Jacques / Hemis.fr 86tl, Heritage Image Partnership Ltd / Peter Thompson 54, Stephen Hughes 127, Image Professionals GmbH / Holger Leue 72t, Image Professionals GmbH / Katharina Jaeger 100, Image Professionals GmbH / LOOK-foto 16tl, imageBROKER / Klaus Rein 130, imageBROKER / Mara Brandl 36cl, 95t, imageBROKER / Marc Rasmus 108, imageBROKER / Martin Moxter 38b, imageBROKER / Moritz Wolf 105b, imageBROKER / Tolo Balaguer 61b, imageBROKER.com GmbH & Co. KG / . / . 16cra, imageBROKER.com GmbH & Co. KG / Martin Moxter 107, imageimage 56, Imago 42–43, Eric James 24t, Jon Arnold Images Ltd / Doug Pearson 50t, LademannMedia 123b, Lanmas 9tl, José María Barres Manuel 30cl, mauritius images GmbH / Gerhard Wild 113t, mauritius images GmbH / Hans Blossey 122, mauritius images GmbH / Klaus-Gerhard Dumrath 25, mauritius images GmbH / Rainer Mirau 133, Perry van Munster 78t, Gianni Muratore 81t, Nature Picture Library / Adrian Davies 72b, Sérgio Nogueira 55t, Nathaniel Noir 19, 99, peterforsberg 15t, robertharding / Markus Lange 75b, Pep Roig 74, Allard Schager 62–63t, Gillian Singleton 77t, StockFood Ltd. / Feiler Fotodesign 83t, Stephen Taylor 32b, Paolo Trovò 132, Westend61 70, Tim Wright 35, Zoonar / AnnaReinert 124b, Zoonar / Bartomeu Balaguer Rotger 13bl, Zoonar / Tolo Balaguer 82b.

AWL Images: Jon Arnold 12crb, 13cl (8), 65b, 93, Davide Camesasca 5, 66–67b, Stefano Politi Markovina 129b, Chris Mouyiaris 68–69b, Christian Mueringer 71t.

Banana Club: 118.

Bridgeman Images: Index Fototeca © Successió Miró / ADAGP, Paris and DACS London 2024 28.

Cala Gran Cocktail Bar: 126.

Cuit, Palma: 101.

Depositphotos Inc: Balate Dorin 46–47t.

Dorling Kindersley: Colin Sinclair 34.

Dreamstime.com: Aldorado10 114–115b, Allard1 21tr, 36–37b, 64b, Artesiawells 62b, 91b, Iigo Arza Azcorra 37tr, Maciej Bledowski 44–45b, Philippe Demande 16ca, Zigmunds Dizgalvis 12cr, 103b, Dorinmarius 20br, 26–27b, Dudlajzov 27tr, 51b,

A NOTE FROM DK

The rate at which the world is changing is constantly keeping the DK travel team on our toes. While we've worked hard to ensure that this edition of Mallorca is accurate and up-to-date, we know that opening hours alter, standards shift, prices fluctuate, places close and new ones pop up in their stead. So, if you notice we've got something wrong or left something out, we want to hear about it.Please get in touch at travelguides@dk.com

Within each Top 10 list in this book, no hierarchy of quality or popularity is implied. All 10 are, in the editor's opinion, of roughly equal merit.

Penguin
Random
House

First edition 2003

Published in Great Britain by Dorling
Kindersley Limited, DK, 20 Vauxhall Bridge Road,
London SW1V 2SA

The authorised representative in the EEA is
Dorling Kindersley Verlag GmbH. Arnulfstr.
124, 80636 Munich, Germany

Published in the United States by DK Publishing,
1745 Broadway, 20th Floor, New York, NY 10019, USA

The publishers cannot accept responsibility for any consequences
arising from the use of this book, nor for any material on third
party websites, and cannot guarantee that any website address
in this book will be a suitable source of travel information.

A CIP catalog record for this book
is available from the British Library.

A catalog record for this book is available
from the Library of Congress.

ISSN: 1542 1554
ISBN: 978 0 2417 1886 5

Printed and bound in China

www.dk.com

MIX
Paper | Supporting
responsible forestry
FSC™ C018179

This book was made with Forest
Stewardship Council™ certified
paper – one small step in DK's
commitment to a sustainable future.
Learn more at **www.dk.com/uk/
information/sustainability**